BEING WITH

BEING WITH

Book 1 THE CORE COURSE

Exploring life and faith together

Samuel Wells

CANTERBURY
PRESS

© Samuel Wells 2025

First published in 2025 by the Canterbury Press Norwich

Editorial office
3rd Floor, Invicta House
110 Golden Lane
London EC1Y 0TG, UK
www.canterburypress.co.uk

Canterbury Press is an imprint of Hymns Ancient & Modern Ltd
(a registered charity)

Hymns Ancient & Modern® is a registered trademark of
Hymns Ancient & Modern Ltd
13A Hellesdon Park Road, Norwich,
Norfolk NR6 5DR, UK

All rights reserved. No part of this publication may be reproduced,
stored in a retrieval system, or transmitted,
in any form or by any means, electronic, mechanical,
photocopying or otherwise, without the prior permission of
the publisher, Canterbury Press.

Samuel Wells has asserted his right under the Copyright, Designs and
Patents Act 1988 to be identified as the Author of this Work

British Library Cataloguing in Publication data

A catalogue record for this book is available
from the British Library

ISBN: 978 1 78622 691 4

EU GPSR Authorised Representative
LOGOS EUROPE, 9 rue Nicolas Poussin, 17000, LA ROCHELLE, France
E-mail: Contact@logoseurope.eu

No part of this book may be used or reproduced in any manner for the
purpose of training artificial intelligence technologies or systems.

Typeset by Regent Typesetting

Contents

Being With Resources QR Code — vi
Preface — vii

Part 1 Foundations — 1

1 First Principles — 3
2 The Eight Dimensions — 11
3 Underlying Ethos — 16

Part 2 Approach — 23

1 Structure — 25
2 Method — 41
3 Formation — 55

Part 3 Courses and Commentary — 63

1 The Being With Course — 65
2 Commentary on Talks — 92
3 Commentary on Wonderings — 112
4 Being With Global — 127

The Impact of Being With — 153
References and Further Reading — 164

Scan the QR code below to access the Being With resources:

- Access to the live training, an essential to helping with the delivery of Being With.
- Support videos.
- Downloadable resources including advertising posters, postcards and banners.
- The latest ever-growing online resource library.
- Monthly update emails.

being-with.org/book1/

Preface

The Being With course is a ten-week enquirers' programme for groups of people who are new to Christianity, considering returning after a period away, or looking to embrace a broader theological outlook than that with which they may perhaps have been previously familiar. The course is a statement of faith that the Holy Spirit works in our lives and that in Jesus' story we behold God's gift of and pattern for abundant life. It's also an attempt to align the way we encounter and practise Christianity as closely as possible with the content of the faith itself. This book is an introduction to the ethos and methods of the course and a presentation of the materials needed to run a course, together with commentary. It's an expanded edition of *Being With: A Course Exploring Christian Faith and Life: Leaders' Guide*. In addition to the original course, this volume also includes Being With Global, a version of the course intended for those for whom English is not a preferred language, for younger age-groups, and for any who prefer somewhat simpler terminology.

The original Being With course was a group at St Martin-in-the-Fields for exploring faith created by Sally Hitchiner and me, which first met in January 2020. It went online in lockdown and proliferated during the pandemic. It spread back in-the-room as conventional meeting patterns resumed in 2022. Since then, it's been practised both in-the-room and online. Two books, *Being With: A Course Exploring Christian Faith and Life: Leaders' Guide* and *Being With: A Course Exploring Christian Faith and Life: Participants' Companion* were published in 2022. James Fawcett began as Head of Being With in 2022. He has done an outstanding job of building an international network of trained leaders and participating congregations such that many thousands of people new to, returning to, re-evaluating and seeking enrichment in faith are now 'graduates' of the original Being With course in many countries, particularly the UK and the US. He has now a close involvement in the movement and a level of experience in running courses and training leaders that goes well beyond mine, and his reflections and insights on all aspects of the course have enriched and enhanced this second edition.

The Being With course arose from four sources. One was a long-standing sense that churches across a broad spectrum of theological and liturgical traditions are generally less attuned to what's involved in bringing people to faith than evangelical ones, and generally need to up their game in this area. Another was my theological exposition of 'being with', beginning in 2011 with the publication of *Living Without Enemies*, and explored in several books, the best known of which are *A Nazareth Manifesto* (2015), *Incarnational Ministry* (2017) and *Incarnational Mission* (2018). Being With began as a way of reimagining mission, but has expanded to become a project for reinterpreting the whole of Christian theology, as fully articulated in *Constructing an Incarnational Theology* (2025). A third was Sally Hitchiner's extensive background in leading and promoting enquirers' courses and her energy and imagination for how such a culture could be translated into a different setting. And the fourth was the particular culture of St Martin-in-the-Fields in central London, a community where faith and action have long been held close together, and where initiatives that have benefited the wider church and world have long found fertile soil. While this volume bears my name, I want to give great credit to Sally, without whose inspiration there wouldn't be a Being With course and movement, and James, who has with great skill organized, garnered funds for, extended and empowered the movement. I also want to celebrate the now myriad numbers of leaders and participants whose engagement and enthusiasm have made this now an international movement.

Much of the material in this book has appeared in different forms elsewhere. The published sources of the talks are noted in the commentary. Some of the introductory material, especially that which seeks to summarize my previous publications, has been adapted from various published sources. I present it here to assist those seeking to understand

PREFACE

the course better without having to read large numbers of books. Needless to say, to gain a fuller understanding of the theological convictions and catechetical ethos of the course, the books quoted are the most obvious place to go. For further courses beyond the original course, see *Being With: Courses for Living*.

The course would not be what it is without countless participants and leaders, administrators and trainers, whose wisdom and insight constitute the course as much as the materials found in this volume. Some of their feedback is recorded at the end of this book.

Part 1
Foundations

1

First Principles

The Being With course is based on three principles. All are convictions about God (theology) that translate into principles about our action (ethics). The first is about Jesus, the second about the Holy Spirit, and the third about the Father.

I

The first principle is that *God created the universe to be with us in Christ*. God is Trinity – Father, Son and Holy Spirit in perfect relationship. The persons of the Trinity don't need to solve one another's problems or overcome adversity together: theirs is a perpetual condition of being with. Their mutual relationships are characterized by attention, mystery, delight, participation, enjoyment and glory. The dynamic behind existence is that the Trinity desired to be in relationship beyond itself: humankind is the name for that with which the Trinity desired to be in relationship. The form that relationship takes is Jesus. Jesus is fully human, fully divine: God and humankind in utter relationship.

Thus the incarnation is a doctrine prior to creation – because if God had held no desire to be in relationship with humankind, there would have been no creation. Incarnation is the reason for creation. Jesus came to embody God's desire to be in relationship with us. In his life he shows us what being with means. It means forming faithful community. It means making relationships of dignity and grace with outcasts and the oppressed. It means challenging those who misuse power. In his death,

BEING WITH: FOUNDATIONS

Jesus shows us that nothing will divert God from the determination to be with us, whatever befall. In his resurrection we behold that nothing can thwart this divine purpose. At Pentecost we see how God empowers us to be with Jesus always. Ultimately on the Last Day existence will cease and we and all creation will be drawn into God's essence and dwell with God, ourselves, one another and the renewed creation for ever. Being with will be all in all.

This is a different story from the one Christianity has most often told. This is not a story about a human predicament caused by a catastrophic human fall from grace and the generous act of God in sending the Son to rescue us by sacrifice, substitution or example. That's a story that runs from fall to cross. This is a much bigger story that begins before creation and ends after the end of time – indeed never ends. Jesus' incarnation – his 33 years among us – is not a detour God took into human existence to set a few things straight before returning to majesty, might and magnificence on high; instead, those 33 years show us the true character of God more truly than we'd ever seen it before or have ever seen it since. Jesus comes among us to embody God's realm: and God's realm means humans in true and utter relationship with God, themselves, one another and the creation. Jesus' ministry displayed God's realm in luminous words, prophetic gestures and transformational relationships. The fact that humanity had strayed far from the realm Jesus embodied resulted in him being executed in a ghastly manner. But even as he was being executed, he embodied utter relationship with us – even jeopardizing his relationship with his Father. And in his resurrection, we see that his relationships with God, us and the creation are ultimately unbreakable. The way God is with us in Christ is the way God will be with us for ever.

The ethical implication of this theological claim is that, every time we embody this being with, we fulfil the original purpose of Trinity, incarnation and creation, and anticipate the ultimate destiny of all created things. We are, in short, living as we were intended to live and as we are called to live. So a Being With course isn't simply a forum in which to discover information about what Christianity claims: it's an actual experience of what those claims describe, and a training in how to embody those claims elsewhere.

FIRST PRINCIPLES

Christianity is not a message or a set of convictions detachable from the shape of Jesus' life or the way the gospel is communicated; Christianity precisely *is* a form of relationship – with God, ourselves, one another and the creation – and an introduction to the faith needs to embody what that relationship looks and feels like. Thus everything that takes place on the course should be crafted to be an experience of relationship and an experience of God's realm. Participants shouldn't think at the end of the course, 'Ok, I quite enjoyed that. Now I should go and find out what Christianity and the church are really like.' Instead, they should look back on the ten weeks together and realize, 'That was Christianity. That was church. That was what it means to be with God and one another.'

The Christian faith is not a fuel that fills up a vehicle, whereupon the driver says, 'Just you watch me when I go.' It's a fundamental disposition towards God and one another, and the way to inhabit it is not to talk about it as an abstract idea but to experience it as something already all around you. Jesus isn't an instrument God uses to achieve something more important than Jesus. Jesus *is* the more important thing – because Jesus embodies God utterly with us, and us utterly with ourselves, one another and the creation. Likewise this course isn't a method to bring about something more important beyond it. The course is *an experience of that beyond* – full relationship with God and one another. But because that's a bit scary for some, the course is carefully designed so this doesn't become apparent till the simple enjoyment of discovering more about oneself and each other is well under way.

II

The second principle of the course is that *the Holy Spirit has been at work in the lives of each of the participants since those lives began.* This is a conviction about the sovereignty of God. The Holy Spirit is constantly seeking to be in relationship with each one of us. That relationship is not an all-or-nothing thing. We can look back and say, 'The Holy Spirit was with me, urging, discouraging, inspiring, redirecting, lamenting, restoring, every step of the way, even though now I realize how much I was

BEING WITH: FOUNDATIONS

trying to push that relationship away.' It's true that God is fundamentally different from us. God is essence – for ever. We are existence – time-bound, space-limited, of temporary duration and restricted capacity. God is creator; we are creatures. But Jesus' incarnation, if we allow it to be the definitive thing we know about God, overcomes that entire and comprehensive difference. It shows that God and humanity can find a point of correspondence.

The Holy Spirit names the ways God makes Christ present in the mundane seasons and extraordinary moments of our lives. The purpose of this course is to enable participants not only to discern the presence of the Holy Spirit in their lives to this point, but to begin to articulate the effect of that presence, and thus be more confident in using the language of faith and making it their own. The course seeks to enable people to become used to discerning the ways God works, and how those ways translate into the role of God's hand in their life – past, present and future. It's not so much, 'I want to be a Christian so God can start to work in me.' It's more, 'I realize now how much I've resisted the Holy Spirit's work in the world and in my life to this point, and I now want to be a willing partner in everything the Holy Spirit is bringing about.'

One way to describe this is that the course is working with an *asset model* of how God transforms us. A deficit model would suggest seekers and the lapsed are empty vessels, waiting to be filled with revelation that can only come from the leaders. Alternatively it would assume the participants are in a state of total depravity, unable to will the good until the Spirit infuses them and they cooperate through a declaration of faith. Neither of these models does full justice to the centrality of Christ's incarnation for understanding who God is and who we are. When God came into intimate face-to-face relationship with us, God didn't reject our humanity, but assumed our humanity, and built upon it in Jesus. In the incarnation Jesus didn't expect us to come to him. *He became what we are.* He didn't assume we had to be transformed in order to be in relationship with him: he related to us, fully and utterly, as we are. God's approach to being with us isn't to start from zero, erasing all our earnest and honest efforts and making all the running without us. Grace doesn't eradicate nature, but perfects it.

FIRST PRINCIPLES

The course assumes God has already given us everything we need to be in relationship. And what we're called to is a fourfold relationship – with God, with ourselves, with one another and with the creation. In this spirit the course builds on the revelation the participants have already received. It doesn't pretend they are 'anonymous Christians' or already within the sheepfold. But it does perceive the work of the Holy Spirit as no more active in the believer than the seeker, the lapsed, those of no professed faith, those of another faith, or even the hostile. The Holy Spirit was, after all, at work in Judah and his brothers as they threw Joseph into the pit – and may even have been at work in Judas. The pivotal moment in the Joseph story comes at the end, where Joseph says to his brothers that what they meant for evil, God meant for good (Gen. 50.20).

What this means is that we're not interested in atheism, if atheism is a catalogue of things you don't believe. We're interested in faith. I always say, 'Don't tell me what you don't believe; tell me what you *do* believe.' That changes the conversation. Because everyone believes in something, regardless of whether they recognize what Christians call God. Everyone has some guiding principle for their life; some trust in relationships, others in scientific conclusions, others again in their own lived experience, others again in noble ideals of freedom or justice. The Being With course doesn't demolish these things: instead it seeks to build on them.

III

The third principle of the course is that *the Father's means and the Father's ends are identical.* There is no detour via which God must adopt tactics or strategies contrary to the ways the persons of the Trinity mutually indwell and embrace each other. This is a point that newcomers to Christianity, and indeed especially children, often grasp more instinctively than established Christians. 'If God loves everybody, why is there so much smiting of the Amalekites? Why does Elijah have to slaughter all 450 prophets of Baal? Why are 75,000 people killed at the end of the book of Esther?' All these are good questions. But some questions are even more far-reaching. 'If the Father is all-powerful, why does saving us require sacrificing the Son? How can we be sure the Father loves us if loving the Son means requiring him to go to the cross? How can we anticipate experiencing joy in heaven if we are to suppose others are sent to eternal hell?' All of these questions point to inconsistency in God's character – an inconsistency that inhibits trust, on which all true faith must rest, and that suggests inequality, unfairness and injustice, let alone bloodthirsty and savage inclinations, all of which seem incompatible with grace and truth.

The principle that the Father's means and the Father's ends are identical puts positively the profound and appropriate conviction that causes such questions to surface. How could it possibly be otherwise? Yet the church has long countenanced an account of the gospel that included portrayals of God's character that contravene this principle and suggest a divine being whose purposes and methods seem far from admirable. By seeking in Jesus the utter and trustworthy embodiment of the Father's character and purpose, this course refocuses this crucial question.

Throughout the story, the incarnate Jesus – who is the reason for creation, anticipated in covenant, made present by the Spirit, dwelling with us in glory – exercises entire congruence between who he is and what he does; why he does it and how he does it. He comes as a tiny child – utterly with, to the point, remarkably, of almost complete dependence. He grows as a youth, still with, known chiefly by his dialogue with the teachers in the temple (Luke 2.46, a moment that discloses who he is, what he embodies, and whom he is called to be with). He teaches and trains disciples, still with, there being no place to lay his head (Matt. 8.20). He is with the curious and the desperate, the sex worker and the collaborator, until he is arrested, and forced into a crisis where it seems he cannot continue to be with both the Trinity and humankind (Mark 15.34). Beyond this moment, in his resurrection he is once again with both the Trinity and all creation. In his ascension he returns to be with the Trinity, promising to be with his disciples always (Matt. 28.20), an undertaking fulfilled by the events of Pentecost. It is, throughout, a continuous story of with. There is utter, undeviating consistency of purpose and conduct. God does not change character to pull off some necessary activity to secure or guarantee something other than God. God is with;

FIRST PRINCIPLES

creates to be with; is with in Christ; is with despite all challenges; is with in Christ through the Holy Spirit; and will be with us and the renewed creation in Christ and the Holy Spirit for ever.

Where this becomes a point of difference with other introductions to Christianity is that the Being With course does not work with a theory of the atonement, by which Jesus reconciles God and humankind from an enmity or alienation that goes back to the fall. Atonement theories invariably fail to align God's means and God's ends, distorting the character of God by opposing the Father to the Son in some scheme of egregious punishment. They tend to disregard Jesus' life and resurrection and concentrate solely on his death, rendering unclear the significance of the one who went to the cross. Atonement theories generally assume a working-for model of God's activity that obscures God's purpose to be with, and perceives working for as God's assigned role, in ways that make any transition to other forms of relationship in eternity unachievable. After all, in eternal life there is no working for to do. And if that were not enough, such theories tend to pay little or no attention to the fact that, for all their drama and conviction, the world seems as full of sin and evil as ever, suffering abides despite human efforts to suppress it, and death has not lost its dominion: in short, if the aim was to reverse the effects of the fall, those effects appear to be still in full swing.

The aim of a Being With course is not to persuade participants to adopt a theory of the atonement and thereby accept Jesus as the means of their rescue from guilt and mortality. It is to give participants such a profound experience of being with themselves and one another that they begin to comprehend God's desire to be with them now and for ever and to transform their lives into ones in which they are joyfully, consciously and intentionally with God, themselves, one another and the wider creation. The ethics of this is that, if we believe the Father's means and the Father's ends are identical, we become people whose ends and means are likewise intentional.

One of the complexities of the Being With course is the diversity of backgrounds participants bring and of reasons people join a course. The course is designed for those new to Christianity. It's naive to assume people bring no baggage, from life or attitudes to religion. But the course

BEING WITH: FOUNDATIONS

is designed to introduce the language of Christian faith within the framework of being with. However, many people join a course because they are returning to faith having had a period of time away. In many cases that time away was caused by a difficult or painful experience of faith or church. This can inevitably shape a participant's attitude to the material, and some may be quick to judge or reject some parts of the course if they sound too similar to what has caused pain in the past. It's sometimes a challenge to encourage such people to stay with the course and see for themselves what the differences may prove to be. It can also be a challenge to prevent such an agenda dominating the discussion time if profoundly felt by one or more participants. A similar reason for joining may be to investigate a kind of Christianity significantly different from a conservative theological and ethical model with which some have grown tired. Those from such a place often enjoy the course very much – but it can be valuable to remember the course wasn't originally designed for them; so it may not address all of their concerns. Every group is different. Part of non-anxious leadership is to trust the group to find its own way, even if one or two of the early sessions may at times feel uncomfortable.

2

The Eight Dimensions

Being with is a concept and a practice with extensive theological, ethical, missiological, pastoral and devotional aspects. Since I began exploring these aspects seriously in 2008, I have published many books exploring these different avenues. I maintain that, while most of the world assumes the human problem is limitation – that our lives are limited in length, our bodies limited in capacity, or world limited in resources – in fact our real problem is isolation. What inhibits us is our alienation from one another, the wider creation, and God. The paradox of our existence is twofold: we keep trying to overcome limitation, with the result we neglect the real problem; and many of our efforts to overcome limitation in fact result in increasing isolation – for example technology that means we can communicate across the world while meanwhile we don't know our neighbour's name.

I then delineate four ways of addressing our human problems. *Working for* assumes people are defined by their predicaments, and the most direct and compassionate way to interact is to use one's skills to resolve those predicaments for them. Working for requires one to cultivate and enhance one's skills and shape one's compassion to be alert for opportunities to use those skills to make other people's lives better. It is full of activity (working). But crucially it makes with secondary and dispensable. It doesn't necessarily involve conversation, understanding or mutuality. It is action without relationship.

Working with, like working for, is focused on active steps to overcome problems (working). But unlike the previous assumption of acting on another person's behalf, it seeks in every way to make the project a collaborative exercise, not just with the person encountered but with a wider

BEING WITH: FOUNDATIONS

range of people experiencing the same or a similar plight. Working with is not fundamentally about developing one's own skills to a point where one can rectify other people's problems. It's about facilitating a partnership between two or more people, where each has significant and valuable contributions to bring to the business in hand. It's about the momentum and solidarity generated through addressing a problem together.

The third form of engagement is *being with*. Being with is different from working for because it focuses on the relationship itself (with) rather than perceiving primarily or wholly its instrumental value. But being with differs also from working with, because it requires a focus on enjoying the person and growing through what they truly are (being), rather than assuming the encounter is an opportunity to exercise one's agency in bringing about change. Being with thus requires a transformation of heart and mind from conventional forms of encounter. It's not about solving problems. It's about enjoying relationship for its own sake.

The fourth kind of encounter, *being for*, isn't really a form of encounter at all, because it doesn't require you to have any actual conversation with another person. You don't need to know anything about them; instead, you judge things entirely from the perspective of a righteous observer. Like being with, you don't yourself actually bring about any tangible change. But unlike being with, neither do you develop a mutually respectful, reciprocally upbuilding relationship with a person; you simply assume you know what they are seeking and advocate their imagined cause on their behalf. Unlike working for or working with, you assume others should be called upon to bring change about. It is not for you to do so: your role is to identify what's wrong, decry the failures of the world, and describe what should be done. In an information-saturated age of capturing attention by offering vivid instant judgements, it's probably the most common model of the four.

It will be clear among these four ways of addressing human problems, two risk increasing isolation, while only two significantly position themselves to reduce it. These two are working with and being with – the common factor being the word 'with'. I call 'with' the most important word, precisely because it addresses the fundamental human predicament. I then examine the shape of Jesus' life according to these categories.

THE EIGHT DIMENSIONS

If one takes a traditional view of his ministry, he spends perhaps a week in Jerusalem working for us – dying and rising for the sake of the world. He spends perhaps three years in Galilee working with us – empowering disciples, teaching about the kingdom, demonstrating the ways of God. But he spends fully 30 years simply being with us: the hidden years, largely in Nazareth. The percentages – 1 per cent working for, 10 per cent working with, 90 per cent being with – reveal God's priorities. Those who follow Jesus must surely say, 'These are my priorities, too.' The paradox is that the church's mission has tended to reverse these percentages and see its role as largely working for. As we've seen above, its theological assumptions have likewise been to perceive God fundamentally through the lens of working for – as the one whose role is to fix our human predicament. This course outlines a different vision for God and for us.

The next question is, precisely what does being with entail? I answer this question by outlining eight dimensions of being with. They are as follows.

- The first is *presence*, which seems obvious until you realize that neither working for nor being for necessarily require presence: they can often operate from a safe distance. Presence means being in the same physical space as the person with whom you are engaging.
- Next comes *attention*, which turns generality into particularity and transforms 'showing up' into focused interaction. Attention requires one to harness concentration, memory, emotion, intellect, gaze, scrutiny, wonder and alertness here and nowhere else, directly and without mediation.
- Then there is *mystery*. This rests on distinguishing between a problem, which has a generic quality, can be perceived equally well by anybody, can be addressed from the outside, and can be solved using skills acquired elsewhere, and a mystery, which is unique, can't be fixed or broken down into its constituent parts, is not fully apparent to an outsider, but can only be entered, explored and appreciated.
- Lest all this seem too solemn and earnest, the fourth dimension is *delight*. This is the recognition of abundance where conventional engagement is inclined only to see deficit. Delight rejects the template

of how things should be, and opens itself to surprise, humour, subversion and playfulness. Delight is glad to take time where conventional engagement is overshadowed by urgency.
- The next two dimensions are in some ways a pair. *Participation* names the way with is indispensable and unsubstitutable. It diverts attention from what is done to ensuring the right balance of who does it. Of the hundred reasons to bypass being with, efficiency is near the top of the list. Participation says there's no justification for leaving someone behind, and queries whether our hurry to get somewhere is rooted in our reluctance truly to engage with the person with whom we are travelling.
- By contrast *partnership* is more prepared to see how respective gifts can, when appropriately harnessed, together enable a team to reach a common goal. Partnership sees how the gifts of the 'needy' person, habitually obscured by the working-for impulse to be helpful on one's own terms, can make unique contributions to common projects. In this sense it comes within the territory of working with, and indicates how much working with and being with sometimes overlap.
- The dimension that encapsulates and epitomizes all the previous ones is *enjoyment*. This rests on Augustine's distinction between what we use, which runs out and is a means to some further end, and what we enjoy, which is of value for its own sake, an end in itself. Being with, simply put, is enjoying people whom the world, having no use for, is inclined to discard.
- Finally, *glory* names the purpose of all things: the opening words of John's Gospel ('the Word became flesh ... and we have seen his glory', 1.14) demonstrate that the epitome of glory, and the originating purpose and final goal of all things, is God being with us in Christ.

Each of these dimensions is rooted in the life of the Trinity and embodied in the life of Jesus. Jesus extends to humankind the quality of being with that characterizes the relations of the persons of the Trinity with each other.

These eight dimensions are a description of how a Being With course should be conducted and what its results should be. The means and

THE EIGHT DIMENSIONS

the ends are identical. In my wider writings I have explored how these dimensions play out in a host of discipleship, ministry and mission contexts – in our lives, in the church and in the world. In the book *Being With: Courses for Living*, the tenth and final course, entitled Being With Being With, is an introduction to these eight dimensions in the form of a Being With course, with two introductory sessions followed by one session devoted to each dimension.

Thus the original Being With course is an introduction not only to the Christian faith but to a lifestyle and ethic that covers every aspect of our relationships with ourselves, one another, the world at large and the wider creation, in a spirit of 'living God's future now' – that is, behaving today in a way that anticipates the way we will be with God for ever.

3

Underlying Ethos

There are a number of other concepts from my experience and writing that play a significant role in the approach taken in the Being With course, and I offer an overview here to facilitate greater understanding of what the course is and what it's seeking to do.

I

Linked to my argument that the world assumes our human problem is limitation is an assertion that the world (and the church) is captivated by a myth of scarcity. We assume there's not enough information, resources, wisdom, knowledge. In a theological vein, we assume there's not enough revelation – the Bible and human experience don't yield enough truth or insight into the ways of the divine. My sense is that what lies at the bottom of this is the unspoken assumption that there's not enough God – that God is insufficient in presence, in action, in manifestation, in care, or even in substance itself. By contrast my argument is that there's actually too much God: our problem isn't that God is not enough for us, but that God is in fact too much for us. We're overwhelmed. And, being overwhelmed, we quickly set about putting up barriers to being drowned by the too-much God, much as we would put our forearms in front of our eyes in the face of a dazzling light. What that means is that we become habituated in turning away the gifts God sends – so much so that we end up experiencing life as scarcity. We are easily threatened when we fear being overwhelmed by gifts, and it becomes second nature to turn gifts

UNDERLYING ETHOS

away. So we fail to realize that God is giving us everything we need; and instead we bewail that we don't have enough.

I use this argument in many settings: about the so-called 'decline' of the church; about the church's difficulty in receiving gifts such as the ministry of women and the contribution of people who are LGBTQ+; about the country's struggle with seeing the gift of asylum seekers and refugees; and many other contexts. I explore the argument in detail in *God's Companions: Reimagining Christian Ethics*. It also forms a key component, especially in the first session, in Being With the Other, a course that can be found in *Being With: Courses for Living*. This notion of abundance is key to understanding the Being With course. I said earlier that the Holy Spirit has been at work in the lives of each of the participants since those lives began. What this statement implies in the context of abundance is that God has already given the participants everything they need to come to faith. Of course we hope they'll have profound experiences together in this course. But the most significant thing that happens is that they come to realize the abundance of their lives where they may previously only have perceived scarcity – certainly as far as revelation is concerned. What takes place in the response to the wonderings is an experience of scarcity being reconfigured as abundance. What takes place as elements of the responses are integrated into the talk is that participants perceive how revelation is an extended, elaborate and ordered exposition of experiences like their own. They realize the significance of their long-suppressed or forgotten experiences and receive the gift of the whole revelation cherished by the church.

II

In addition to *God's Companions*, another key text in my early work is *Improvisation: The Drama of Christian Ethics*. In this work I highlight the challenge that life continues to present novel and unpredictable challenges the scriptures don't explicitly anticipate. I note the problems with thinking of the Bible as a script that we as actors perform. One is the common misconception that Christianity is about recreating a golden era when disciples once got the story right. Instead I propose several themes from theatrical improvisation as a way of understanding the Christian life today.

Jeremiah portrays God as a potter who finds the clay spoiled in his hands and refashions it into another vessel. This is a simple picture of God as improviser, committed neither to discard nor destroy creation or Israel, but to keep the story going through creative adaptation. Scripture offers countless models of improvisation. In particular the Old Testament account of the Exile and the New Testament account of the Acts of the Apostles provide sustained studies in how the people of God may draw on long-practised habits to act in new circumstances.

I have previously defined improvisation in the theatre as 'a practice through which actors seek to develop trust in themselves and one another in order that they may conduct unscripted dramas without fear'. Improvisation is not about being clever, witty, spontaneous or original. Theatrical improvisers find they have to overcome such urges, which in fact kill the drama. Instead they must learn to be obvious, rely on in their learned habits, and trust and enjoy one another. Improvisation may be funny, but it's not thereby trivial or self-indulgent. It is an ordered, skilled and courageous series of practices that offers enormous potential for helping the church become a community of trust that may faithfully encounter the threatening and the unknown.

Already it should be clear how improvisation applies to the Being With course. The course is all about acting in the present – not memorizing a script from the past. The host's role is to keep the story going by creating an atmosphere of trust where all contributions are acceptable and silence is not to be feared. But there are three specific practices within theatrical improvisation that inform the course.

The first is forming habits. Conventional ethics assumes its job is to help people make the right decisions in a crisis. But the real location for living well doesn't lie in the moment of decision: it's invariably too late by then. The crucial issue is the formation of character, which takes a long time and is largely about learning to take the right things for granted. This affects the Being With course profoundly. It is for this reason the course doesn't aim for or aspire to a 'conversion' moment, where a person

UNDERLYING ETHOS

suddenly becomes a Christian. Such things can happen, but they're not what the course is structured around. Instead the course seeks to train its participants in learning to take the right things for granted – such that they gradually start to think and act as Christians, rather than impulsively decide to become one. Likewise the key to being a leader, as we shall see later in this book, is the formation of character. This way of understanding ethics forms part of the course Being With Yourself, which is among those to be found in *Being With: Courses for Living*.

The second practice is known as overaccepting. Whenever a dialogue partner says or does anything, whether friendly, hostile or indifferent, they're making what's known as an 'offer'. You have three options in return. You may 'accept'. This means to accept the premise of the offer and let it shape your subsequent interaction. Or, you may 'block' the offer, by rejecting its premise. The third option is to 'overaccept' the offer. This means to accept the premise of the offer but place the offer within a much larger canvas than had been supposed by the person making the offer. A friend was approached by a sex worker who said, 'Would you like a good time?' To have accepted would have been to have said, 'Yes, how much?' To have blocked would have been to have said, 'No, thank you.' Instead, my friend overaccepted and said, 'I'd like to talk to you. I don't think what you're offering me right now is what I'd call a good time. If I can buy you a drink, I'd like to talk to you about what I would call a *really* good time.' Improvisers seek to train themselves to accept all offers. This seems a terrifying, even foolish commitment. But sometimes blocking is not an option. Sometimes blocking assumes one has access to superior violent force. In many cases violent blocking is futile, even if it seems justified. Overaccepting is especially significant for those who lack sufficient power simply to block threatening offers.

Overaccepting is vital for the whole structure of the course. A key theological insight underlying the course is that the Holy Spirit has already made Christ present to the participants in myriad ways throughout their lives, and this course is an opportunity, quite probably for the first time, for them to identify, recognize, name and come to understand that this is what has been happening. In other words, the whole course is an exercise in placing our own small stories into the large story of what God is doing

BEING WITH: FOUNDATIONS

in the world. And this process is catalysed by observing as other participants are making parallel discoveries. This is the single most significant reason why participants experience the course as a life-changing process. Because they are, in subtle, unthreatening and non-manipulative ways, renarrating their whole lives in just ten 90-minute sessions. It's hardly surprising people say things like, 'This has done what months of therapy failed to do.' It's important to realize the host has simply to trust this process will take place: it's seldom necessary to highlight it, talk about it or expedite it. It just happens. And it happens to everyone together.

The third practice is called reincorporation. Keith Johnstone, in his book *Impro*, describes improvisation as like walking backwards. Instead of walking *forwards* to face the daunting emptiness of an unknown future, the improviser walks *backwards*, seeing discarded material, near or far, as a host of gifts enabling the continuance and resolution of troubling narratives. Reincorporation comes about when discarded elements from earlier in the narrative begin to reappear, especially at moments when redeeming these discarded elements offers the resolution to what seemed insurmountable problems. Children are often highly attuned to reincorporation and refuse to believe they have reached the end of a story until elements and characters earlier set aside finally reappear. Charles Dickens' novels are notable for immense and rapid reincorporation in their closing chapters, where it sometimes seems almost every character in a sprawling narrative comes back into the story in a new way. In the fifth session of the Being With course, the talk explains how Act 5 of the Christian drama is entirely made up of discarded elements from earlier parts of the story. This becomes the key motif in understanding heaven: how God brings back into the story as gift those elements that have previously been suppressed or oppressed as obstructive or superfluous.

Reincorporation takes place in the Being With course most explicitly at the point where the storyteller inserts elements from the responses to the wonderings into the talk. It can be incredibly moving for a person who's shared an apparently trivial or touchingly tender response to hear, just a few minutes later, their contribution being offered back to the whole group as part of the material of revelation. It's like our humanity being taken up into God's divinity in the incarnation: revelation is precisely an

UNDERLYING ETHOS

account of how divine and human coincide and relate. But reincorporation also appears at other moments in the course. It can feature in the welcome, when the host or another participant recalls something shared in an earlier session. It features whenever one participant refers back to a previous participant's response. And it often happens in the discussion time, when host, storyteller or participant may revisit a remark made earlier in the session or the course and now see it in a new light.

III

The part of the course that intrigues most participants from the word go is the wondering. This is something I learned from the late American catechist Jerome Berryman. His extensive Montessori-inspired children's programme Godly Play makes wondering key to the children's response to the story. (It's an innovation of the Being With course to do the wondering before the story.) Berryman is following in the footsteps of Sofia Cavalletti, an Italian who has sought to bring the Montessori tradition into harmony with the trajectory for the Roman Catholic Church set by the Second Vatican Council. Cavalletti's ethos is set out in her book *The Religious Potential of the Child* and is embodied in her children's programme known as the Catechesis of the Good Shepherd. Jerome Berryman, originally a Presbyterian, latterly an Episcopal priest, developed this programme and focused it more on a group of children than an individual child, based it more explicitly on a eucharistic shape, and made it more accessible and adaptable to liturgically formed Protestants.

I first encountered these programmes when I was the vicar of a parish in a neighbourhood experiencing significant social disadvantage. I was leading worship for a congregation, many of whom could read but for whom in general reading was an activity that reminded them of their low social standing. Of those who could and did read for pleasure, many were looking for forms of worship that were sustainable in a context where unsettled children would often wander in and out in the course of a service, sometimes seeking attention in distressing ways. There being little discernible enthusiasm for running a Sunday school during the main act of worship, services were generally all-age. I therefore took to exploring ways in which liturgy, sharing, education and storytelling could come together. I wanted to affirm that worship was a corporate action in which people performed some things repeatedly (and thus came to take them for granted) while remaining open to discover other things for the first time.

I once attended a training session for church children's workers that was full of how to keep children amused and attentive through a multi-day holiday club. A member of the audience asked, 'What do you do if a child asks a question you don't know how to answer?' 'Ah,' said the expert, 'Questions. They can be a problem. The best thing is to put someone in a quiet place over in a corner, someone like the vicar, and you can send the child with a question over to them if you don't want to interrupt the session and you don't know what to say.' This exchange became a defining moment for me. It had evidently not occurred to the expert that the children might be discovering something of or about God that the adults did not already know. I realized that this was what my ministry with children was all about: not keeping them busy for fear they might become bored (with God or with me) or disruptive; but creating spaces where children could genuinely meet God, quite possibly in ways I had never imagined. So much ministry with children and young people is a noble effort to be more interesting than God. But the anxiety to keep the children's attention discloses an underlying fear that God perhaps is not so interesting after all. The key to Cavalletti's vision came when a child asked her, 'How can I meet God for myself?' Such a question puts much busy children's work in the shade.

The Being With course is a recognition that many of these same tendencies apply in the church's work with adults. Foundational to the course is the conviction that adults can meet God for themselves; God does not belong to the clergy or to the church. The question the child asked Sofia Cavalletti became the question on which the Being With course came to be founded: it's a course intended to assist people in meeting God for themselves – indeed to identify, recognize, name and cherish the ways they already have. In the words of Jacob: 'Surely the Lord is in this place – and I did not know it!'

Part 2
Approach

1

Structure

It's time to speak of how these theological convictions work out in practice. The ten sessions of the course all adopt the same fourfold structure.

The ten-session course of 90-minute in-person or video-conference group meetings of six to 14 people has two leaders, one called the host and the other called the storyteller. It follows the same pattern on each occasion: there are four parts to the event.

Welcome

First comes the welcome. During the welcome each person is invited to speak. At the first session the subject is, 'Tell us a little about what brought you here.' Thereafter the aim is to build fellowship, so the invitation is to go as deep as possible yet as briefly as possible: the usual bidding is, 'What's been the heart of your week?' What this question does is not only cut out the need for a long narrative of circumstantial detail, instead going straight to the jugular, but also to focus on the heart – the feelings, impressions and learnings – not just an inventory of dispassionate events or curious coincidences. This question treats each person's week as a project, and thus lifts it out of the mundane and makes it worthy of other people's appreciative scrutiny. Already we have a sense of what's really moving in one another's lives. And unusually, there's no assumption or insistence that what people share needs to be positive or upbeat. It's absolutely fine to say, 'I spent most of the weekend going through the things in my brother's flat: he left everything such a mess when he died,' or, 'This is the weekend my ex has the kids. I always look forward to the

BEING WITH: APPROACH

freedom of being able to do what I like but actually I miss them when they're not here and spend a lot of time feeling sad about everything that's happened.' You don't have to say, 'I got a promotion at work and my boss said, "You're the best colleague I've ever had."' The more real the answers are, the more the whole session opens up to the truth about one another and the truth about God.

This is the only part of the whole session to which we insist everyone contributes, including the host and the storyteller. (Although we try to keep the rule that the host and storyteller don't speak immediately after one another.) It's based on a simple insight of group dynamics that suggests people feel part of the session once they've said something that's been affirmed and cherished by others. So we try to ensure everyone has the chance to do so in the first ten minutes – and if a participant arrives late, we pause whatever's happening (as soon as the person speaking has finished their contribution) to invite them to tell us what's been the heart of their week, before resuming from wherever we were. But there's something more significant going on at the same time. 'What's been the heart of your week?' makes an implicit assumption that each participant has been exposed to revelation in the course of the previous week. This part of each session is designed so that, in listening expectantly to each other's discoveries and sharing their own, they find without realizing it that they are learning to listen. In other words, they are becoming evangelists before they even realize they have a gospel. Usually the host goes first, immediately after the wondering, to get it going, and the storyteller goes last as a prompt to the host to move on to the wonderings – particularly if the host has lost track of who has and who has not responded. The host would normally thank each participant for their contribution, while the storyteller would thank the host for their contribution.

The theological conviction behind this is that as a society and as a church we are captivated by the assumption that our fundamental human problem is limitation. We complain of age, disability, disease, lack of resources; all the while postponing and distracting from our profound fear of the final limitation, death. Meanwhile we celebrate the breakthroughs that announce the overcoming of limitation: the discovery of a vaccine, the breaking of a speed record, the technology that can communicate across the globe. Yet maybe there's something more profound in the human condition than limitation – something that can't be fixed by new technology and is caused not by not having enough but by misusing what we already have. That phenomenon is isolation. When it comes to isolation, we don't need to go looking for a new gadget to solve the problem. Because what we need, we already have: one another. The problem is our inability or unwillingness to be reconciled with one another, which leaves us isolated.

Hence the course is not fundamentally about giving the participants crucial new information that helps them overcome their human limitations; it's about enabling them to develop relationships through which they begin to imagine what life would be like if they no longer faced the horror of isolation – if they truly knew and experienced what it meant to be with. In being with one another they make steps towards being with God, themselves and creation. In other words, finding salvation. The opening part of the Being With course is not about telling people this but enacting it: within ten minutes of the first session, people are well on the way to overcoming isolation. That may sound a bold claim, but the rest of the course should be an extension of what people encounter in the first ten minutes of the first session: that they are deeply cherished, that their thoughts and experiences are not meaningless, but are part of the great reality that we're all seeking, that we are going to discover truth together, and that this is a place where they can trust others to take their search even more seriously than they do themselves. The aim of an enquirers' group isn't primarily to give us new things, but to encourage, enable and empower us to use the ones already available to us.

Wondering

The second part, which usually lasts about 35 minutes, is what we call the wondering. Each session has a theme, but we don't make a big play of introducing the theme. Instead we enter into it experientially.

Wonderings are most people's favourite part of the course. They are a technique embodied in Jerome Berryman's groundbreaking *Godly*

BEING WITH: APPROACH

Play curriculum for children's catechesis. A wondering is not a question. It doesn't have a question mark at the end. It doesn't have a specific response in mind. The key to a wondering is that it draws out a person's experience and imagination: it's not fixated on a right answer, but dwells gently and playfully on each person's latent perception and insight.

It's worth pausing to reflect on what's wrong with the notion of questions. What's wrong is that it creates a hierarchy of knowledge. Questions steer towards the search for factual knowledge. In an enquirers' group setting, participants are often acutely aware of their ignorance about features of faith, theology and scripture about which they assume, often rightly, that others have greater knowledge than themselves. This can quickly become a game in which those with the most extensive vocabulary about churchy things go to the top of the class. The trouble is such things can hinder as much as facilitate the encounter with the Holy Spirit that the course seeks to bring about. And they can introduce a dynamic that distracts from the culture of mutual cherishing and appreciation the course is trying to promote. There's a place for questions in the fourth part of the session – once the talk has established common ground that puts all participants on a more even field. The course isn't about creating the sense of satisfied customers that 'your questions answered' might evoke; it's inviting participants into a dance, in which wondering conveys a sense of awe – of wonder – that takes people to a place they'd never been to before, a depth of reflection that stays with them throughout the week and for a long time after, until it becomes a way of life.

So, for example, in week 5 the theme is the Bible, and the group might wonder as follows: 'Tell me about a story you've loved a long time.' 'Tell me about a story about your family that everyone's heard too many times.' 'I wonder if you've ever felt there was a story that had no place for you.' 'I wonder if you've ever felt there was a story that *did* have a place for you.' Not everyone need respond to each of the wonderings; some participants may have more than one contribution to make. The point is to increase the sense of respectful playfulness, where each participant appreciates and builds on the contribution of the others, like a game of keepy-uppy, where participants gather in a circle and try to keep a ball in the air without using their hands. When it goes well, you can feel people

STRUCTURE

inspired by discovering things about themselves, as well as growing in wonder as others disclose humour, wisdom and surprises.

Part of the secret about wondering is that people can enter on any level they feel comfortable. So if the wondering is, 'I wonder if you've known what it feels like to be set free' (which is in fact the first wondering of the first session), it's perfectly possible to respond, 'I was in the playground. I was eight years old. I was touched on my shoulder and I had to stand still with my legs apart until someone came and crawled through my legs. No one came for a long time. Eventually, someone came and crawled through and I could run again.' But it's also perfectly acceptable to respond, 'It took me five years to find the courage to leave that marriage, and five years to complete the divorce. I'd gone from the frying pan of a miserable childhood to the fire of a violent marriage. At 37, for the first time in my life, I was free.' The amazing thing is that people do offer such an extraordinary range of responses, from the very start of the first session of the course. And some stay silent till near the end and then drop a bombshell on the group about who they really are, in response to a prompt like, 'I wonder what it's like when a close community breaks apart.'

Wondering is a great leveller. It's not about who knows the Bible best. It's not about who's had the most dynamic religious experiences. It's not about who had the wildest life before joining this course. It's not about how sophisticated or coherent your life is outside this group. It's about who's prepared to explore, play and discover things that nobody in the group knew before the session started. It's as much about finding permission to articulate long-forgotten or deeply suppressed things about oneself as about discovering intriguing and fascinating things about one another. It dismantles any attempt to make faith a way of getting one up on other people, by your righteousness of life or breadth of religious knowledge. It elicits people's digested or half-digested experiences, and places them on a broader canvas than they'd previously perceived.

There are two kinds of wondering. 'I wonder …' is about the imagination or the future. It refers to things that might happen, or feelings that may or may not have been in the speaker's experience, but are nonetheless worth exploring. 'Tell about …' concerns things that have happened.

BEING WITH: APPROACH

These are memories and recollections the speaker feels able to share, in some cases for the first time. Such sharing can be dynamic for the speaker as well as those listening. When we think of sharing deeply, we often assume revelations concern salacious or surprising things about a person's past; and indeed there can be all kinds of surprises when people respond to 'Tell about …'. But however much it may take trust to share something from the past, it's still the past. It's actually more intimate to share something that hasn't happened yet you dream will one day happen, or to disclose a feeling or aspiration that's not yet been fulfilled: that way others know something tender that you've set your hopes on. So both kinds of wondering can be profound. But there is almost always a way of responding that's mundane, simple or funny – though the desire to amuse others sometimes comes from an impulse to avoid becoming more vulnerable.

The theological conviction underwriting this process is that God gives us everything we need. Church and society tend to be captivated by scarcity. We feel we don't have enough – enough resources, enough information, enough revelation. Fundamentally, all these concerns crystallize into one: we feel we don't have enough God. By contrast, the conviction behind this course is that we have too much God – and our problem is that we've developed such strong resistances to being overwhelmed by God that we fail to receive the abundance that God gives us. Thus the wonderings are an exercise in receiving God's abundance. We assume scarcity but in fact the Holy Spirit gives us more than enough. We look in the wrong places, and often fail to recognize or refuse to receive the gifts God gives us. This wondering time is an experience of appreciating the depth and extent of the gifts God has already given us in our experience, observation, memory and imagination.

Three important points of technique arise here, to ensure the course embodies its principles and thus offers a true experience of God's realm. The host offers the wonderings. On a video-conference platform they can be pasted into the comments section on the screen. The silence between wonderings is part of the wondering. There's no need to 'keep the conversation going' by being lively or chatty. There's no requirement for everyone to speak. It's vital to appreciate participants may be delving deep into their memories, sometimes reaching very personal and unresolved experiences, and the silence is seldom unresponsiveness but more often participants evaluating whether what they've found is suitable for sharing. Helping the group become comfortable with silences out of which profound things arise is a key part of the host's role.

The host would normally respond at a minimum with, 'Thank you', to signify the remark has been received and heard. This cultivates a culture in the room of consistent response even if the host may vary it slightly for particular responses. It also gives the host the facility to shut down other participants should they be tempted to comment (or fix), while at the same time indicating to others they can now speak. The storyteller performs this role for the host.

Sometimes a member of the group shares something particularly painful or an experience that's not closed but still very much in progress. When this occurs, it can happen that other members seek not to wonder themselves but to comment on the wondering shared – with sympathy, compassion, or even advice. The host may say, 'Thank you for trusting us,' or, 'We appreciate that may not have been easy to share' – and the use of the participant's name can make a helpful difference here; but the host must gently but firmly discourage the other participants from deviating from the wondering by muscling in to rescue the person who's shared deeply. (If the person is so distressed as to need to drop off the call or leave the room, the storyteller can follow them and give them the support they need, leaving the host to continue with the wondering.) It's important to trust the process and stick to the task; sometimes the impulse to console discloses a reluctance to do the real work of wondering together. At the first session, when introducing the practice of wondering, the host may say, 'We don't comment on one another's wonderings, or say "A similar thing happened to me": we simply cherish what the person's said and honour their trust in sharing it.' This point may need reiterating several times over subsequent sessions.

The third subtle but important point of technique is for the host and the storyteller to be careful not to follow one another's remarks with a contribution of their own – but instead to make sure there's at least one participant response before they do so. This is because the dynamic between the host and the storyteller, who in most cases know one another better than any of the participants know anyone else in the group, can dominate the group, flattening other voices and inhibiting the sense of play and delight. The storyteller will probably contribute fewer responses to wonderings than anyone else, partly because the storyteller has seven or eight minutes of speaking still to come, and doesn't want to hog the microphone, and partly because concentrating on responses so as to integrate some into the talk is demanding work. But it's also vital for host and storyteller to appreciate the power they hold in the group: if they both speak to corroborate one another's remarks, it can make it impossible for a participant to articulate a view or story in tension with such a formidable phalanx.

If the wondering has been given the right tone, of gentle but profound playfulness and genuine appreciation, then it will itself have disclosed enough truths to explore for a whole session. But in this course its role is also to set the scene for the talk, in such a way that the talk is covering ground the group has already traversed and appreciated. The time of wondering becomes the backdrop out of which revelation appears.

The Talk

After about 35 minutes of exploration and offering, it's time for the storyteller to speak about one place of wisdom in the Christian tradition. If you had ten talks of 5–10 minutes each to give about Christianity, what would you say? The talks in this course are crafted to take the group on a journey. The direction of that journey is as follows.

The first talk engages with what it means to be human: poised between the past that we cannot change and sometimes oppresses us, and the future that we cannot imagine and sometimes terrifies us. The talk portrays Christianity as liberation from the prison of the past and the fear of the future. Only in such a way can we genuinely live. The talk is really about resurrection, but it hardly mentions resurrection – it's intended to give an experience of what resurrection means. It concludes with a comprehensive understanding of Christianity as faith about the past, hope about

STRUCTURE

the future and love in the present. The impression it's intended to leave is that Christianity is about everything, and about everything being safe in God – but also about me, now, today.

The second talk stretches the canvas as wide as possible. It recognizes the difference between existence, in which we dwell, and essence, which is where God abides. It humbly accepts that there need have been no existence – except that God wanted to be with us. Existence therefore came into being so God could be with us in Christ; and that desire withstood our rejection of Jesus, and will finally be fulfilled when God draws us into essence – when being with will become eternal. This talk stretches the imagination of many. But it makes a statement that this course will take your widest ponderings seriously: it's not an attempt to induce you into commitment, but to honour you by taking your heart-searchings more seriously than you do yourself.

The third talk takes the premise of the second talk, that Jesus is the reason for all things, but brings that premise into the context of the Gospels. Jesus spent time with an accountable community (the disciples), with the poor, and in often heated dialogue with the authorities. This takes away any abstraction or sentimentality from the gospel story and shows why Jesus was killed – because of the threat he posed to the religious and political status quo. It begins to propose what discipleship means – in this case, spending time with those with whom Jesus spent time.

The fourth talk uncompromisingly follows the logic of the third, by pursuing the notion of accountable community as church. Rather than portray church as duty, instead, through the example of the rabbits of *Watership Down*, it demonstrates church as power – the power of a community that realizes God has given it everything it needs, so long as it genuinely puts all the gifts of the community to work. This is the point where participants are invited to realize that the group they belong to is already acting in significant ways as this kind of church.

The fifth talk offers an overview of the Bible as a five-act play. This can be the most difficult session, because it offers the sharpest contrast between those who've had previous experience of Christianity, and in some cases know the scriptures well, and those to whom the whole structure of the Bible is more or less new, and who would struggle to identify whether a given character was from the Old or the New Testament. But again, the emphasis is not on assimilating knowledge, but on learning to find our own place in God's story, and recognizing that the church is in Act Four of a story that didn't finish in the first century.

The sixth talk is perhaps the most distinctive of the ten in this course. It outlines the notions of working for, working with, being with and being for, and identifies how Jesus spent 90 per cent of his time among us being with – 30 years. Having established that being with is fundamental to how God relates to us, to how we will relate to God and one another eternally, and to how therefore we should relate to one another today, the talk goes a little way into exploring the nature of being with, describing the notions of mystery, delight and enjoyment. The participants begin to realize the holistic aspirations of the course and how the group is going through a sustained experience of being with.

The seventh talk often proves to be the pivotal one, because those who have left conservative churches sometimes carry deep misgivings about the way, in conventional portrayals of the atonement, Jesus is instrumentalized as a device to secure human redemption. Having gained an understanding in the previous six sessions of the God who is with us, now the participants discover how the cross, rather than being the definitive moment of for – Christ dying for us – is in fact the ultimate demonstration of with – Christ being with us even to the point of jeopardizing the integrity of the Trinity.

The eighth talk does several things. It continues the work of the third talk in beginning to push the group into putting the insights they've gained into action. It offers a model of how to begin to be with another person, particularly a person from a different social location from oneself. And then it shows how being with one another is good training for being with God, by disclosing that the four parts of the conversation with another person correspond to the four principal parts of prayer.

The ninth talk continues the theme of being with God in prayer by taking up the most vexed question of prayer – how to pray for a person in distress or trouble. Employing the example of a person whose father has dementia, the talk discusses three ways to pray – the prayer of resurrection, the prayer of incarnation and the prayer of transfiguration, as

STRUCTURE

a way of demonstrating how being with transforms every aspect of life and faith.

Finally, the tenth talk is a capstone to the whole course. From the first talk it revisits the resurrection – the final irresistibility of God being with us. From the second and third talks it demonstrates the centrality of Jesus to all things. From the fifth talk it offers a second account of the Bible, this time as a series of themes that all climax in the resurrection. And from the other talks it crystallizes the notion that God being with us is the nature and destiny of humankind. It's designed to be an inspiring summary of everything the course is about.

What makes these talks unique is not just the content – its emphasis on God's primordial desire to be with us in Jesus, and the way it explores the full dimensions of being with for faith and life. More than that, the uniqueness of the talks is the way the storyteller weaves into each one material the participants have offered in the wonderings. Carefully and gently, the storyteller notes how key moments in each talk echo and embody insights in the foregoing responses to the wonderings, so that some or all group members find their lives inscribed into the story of God. The storyteller weaves together the insights shared among the participants, highlighting places where the experience named resonates with a key theme to be communicated.

In the fifth session, for example, talking about Act Five, consummation, the storyteller says, 'This is what it's like to be in a story that *does* have a place for us, a story where a kaleidoscope of identities and histories together make a gloriously diverse beauty.' The storyteller can say, 'As Rachel was saying earlier, this is like the moment in her antenatal class when she realized they were all incredibly different people, but they were each having a baby.' Likewise in Act Four, we get moments in our experience of church that thrillingly anticipate that embracing story, moments when we say that God's realm (or Act Five) breaks into Act Four. The storyteller can say, 'Just like Chloe described, when she and her fiancé were with her nephews, they had a glimpse of what being parents themselves was going to be like.' In Act One, creation, God says to us, 'I made you this way because I wanted one like you,' and the storyteller can say, 'Like Julie was saying, no one knew what to do with her in her primary

BEING WITH: APPROACH

school because they thought her skin colour would rub off.' In Act Two, covenant, or the Old Testament, the storyteller can cite what participants have shared about being part of a community that constantly wonders if it has everything it needs and tells the same stories over and again. 'Brian was telling us about his grandfather, who never stopped reminding us that the family firm almost went bankrupt in 1967.'

It's not easy to do. Even if you've done it many times before, it's a new challenge every time: you have to listen very carefully and recall a good part of what has been said in the wondering time to be able to integrate it into the talk moments later. Partly for this reason, it's easiest not to customize the talks, but to use them verbatim from this book. The important work is not to adapt the talk to your language and idiom, but to integrate information from the wonderings into the talk – not to saturate it, but to introduce four or five references that highlight contributions from participants. When the course takes place online this is more straightforward – you can speak off the screen and add an asterisk as the wonderings take place for where to mention David's grandfather, and where to refer to Beth's falling off the swing. In person it's a little harder, but all the same principles apply: you simply get better with practice and attention.

This is a kind of improvisation. It's grounded in what improvisers in the theatre call overaccepting: that's to say, the larger story of God embraces and envelops the smaller stories of our lives. There's no wrong turn our lives can take that's beyond the Holy Spirit's capacity to weave back into the story. The participants' contributions aren't irrelevant to the gospel; nor do they constitute the gospel on their own; they're overaccepted by the gospel, such that the gospel is illustrated by them. To hear oneself inscribed into God's story like this can, for a participant, be a truly life-changing experience.

Some participants find the talks are quite dense and even a little intimidating. The secret is not to regard them as a list of instructions you have to retain and implement – more like a meditation that affects how you feel. The point is not to recall all the information but to allow the talks to lead you to a place emotionally and imaginatively. They're designed to repay revisiting several times, so making the talks available after the session can be a helpful way of reducing participants' anxiety that they might be expected to remember details. The talks are a different genre from the rest of the 90-minute session: for some the most important; for others, not.

Reflection

The last half hour is the most conventional part of the course. We leave aside the practice of wondering and the discipline of listening to a talk, and each have the opportunity to offer a reflection or ask a question – about the talk, the theme, the course, or just something that's been on our mind, for minutes or decades. The earlier parts of the session have enabled the participants to name their experience, and also to some extent scrutinize or at least explore it; then they have a chance to hear an account of what Christianity entails. Now they can set what their experience yields alongside what Christianity offers and evaluate each in the light of the other.

Often it can be helpful for the host to open the reflection time with some thoughts about how some of the wondering responses resonated with the story for them, giving examples. Besides this, at this point there isn't usually a great deal for the host to do, except ensuring everyone has a chance to contribute, no single person monopolizes the conversation, and each participant knows and feels that their reflection or question, however humble or off-topic it might seem, is still valuable. It can be helpful for the host to start by saying, 'I wonder what you were thinking or feeling as you listened to that talk.' Again, silence is not a problem, but an indication that each participant is placing what the storyteller has said side by side with their own experience, shared or withheld, so each can evaluate this new information in the light of what they already live by. 'How does this fit?' says one. 'What do I do with my feelings about that?' says another. The habit of wondering lingers: once, when I had explained how God does not use us to achieve something beyond us, but truly enjoys us, seeing us as wondrous in ourselves, worth having for our own sake, one member of the group, usually vocal, now unusually quiet, after a silence said, 'I'm wondering what part of me God enjoys the most.' These are precious moments.

In one of the groups, at session seven, we'd been exploring the cross. One participant digested an account of Christ's death drawn out of her own experience of being with and being alone, God's presence and absence, and the way Christ's spreadeagled hands are saying, 'I have set you as a seal upon my arm, to show you love is stronger than death.' Pondering the narrowness of what she'd been told about the cross a decade earlier, and the expansiveness of this new perspective, she broke down in front of the group. Eventually, once all had held her tears, she sputtered out the words, 'Why did no one tell me this before?' She said it twice, once in sadness, again almost in anger. The truth is, no one could have, if they'd not first listened to her life experience and enabled her to fold those insights together with Christ's story like two climbing vines interweaving with one another.

It can be hard but transformative for a participant to realize their experience can give them an insight into the very heart of God. In session six, when it became clear it was all about relationships – all about love, about being with one another – in the end one participant got angry: 'Don't talk to me about love,' he retorted. 'How's that supposed to relate to me? My partner left years ago, my family live miles away, and my beloved dog just died ... I loved that dog. Where's my love to go now?' he almost shouted. 'Where's my love to go? Tell me that.' How to respond – but to take a risk, and reply, gently, 'Think of it this way. Imagine eternity from God's point of view. Imagine God having all love pent up like you have right now. But God's got that love all pent up potentially for ever. Like you, God's thinking, "Where's my love to go?" So God creates the universe. But God's still got more love to give. So God creates life, and makes humanity, and calls a special people. But God's still got more love to give. So God comes among us as a tiny baby. Maybe God's words "Where is my love to go?" is the most important question of all time. Because half the answer is the creation of the universe, and the other half is Jesus coming among us. So when you ask yourself, "Where's my love to go?", you're getting an insight into the very heart of God.'

On another occasion there was a conversation that helped us articu-

STRUCTURE

late the second principle of Being With. One participant, despite having joined energetically in the course, voiced her disappointment. 'When', she said, 'are we going to talk about the Holy Spirit?' It wasn't immediately clear to what precisely the question was referring. It transpired that she was expecting a dramatic experience that would lead her into a profound intimacy with God. Hence she was feeling short-changed. When we appreciated what the question meant, we quickly realized what the answer was. It became the focal moment of the whole ten-week course, the big reveal that until that instant we hadn't at all identified as a big reveal. The answer was, 'Don't you see? This *whole course* has been about the Holy Spirit. Not a Holy Spirit who's content to do strange and wonderful things that surprise and delight. But a Holy Spirit who's been acting in your life since the day you were born, a Holy Spirit who's made Christ present to you in friend and stranger, a Holy Spirit who's bestowed on you gifts of love, joy and peace, patience, faithfulness and gentleness. *This whole course* has been tracing how God has been speaking to you all along, how the work of the Holy Spirit in making Christ present is by no means restricted to the church but is revealed in every instance where the kingdom breaks in through acts of generosity, reconciliation and grace. What we've been modelling together is a way of discerning the work and voice of the Holy Spirit, as we've explored our past experience and present imagination and discovered together wisdom and truth. What we've been doing is weaving together the two climbing vines of the Christian story and our story, till we realize we can't perceive one without the other. What we've discovered is not just the way the Holy Spirit breathes through the Bible, the Eucharist, prayer and baptism, but how the Holy Spirit humbles the church by speaking through the stranger, the outcast, the overlooked and the lowly. Don't you think that's pretty exciting?' There was an embarrassed, shuffly silence.

What that transformative conversation disclosed was what the Being With course was seeking to communicate to that young woman: 'The Holy Spirit has been working in you from the day your life began – whether or not you've been aware of it. And that sense of the heart of your week and those wonderings that you shared are exactly the ways in which we begin to discern how the Holy Spirit has been working and

BEING WITH: APPROACH

what it's been up to.' "Surely the Lord is in this place and I never knew it." "Did we not feel our hearts on fire?" "You have searched me and known me, and you have perceived my thoughts from afar."' This is why leading the course is so rewarding. It's an experience of how the Spirit works to transform church through kingdom and thus to give us glimpses of for ever now.

Fundamentally the work of the Holy Spirit is to make Christ present among us. The four parts of each Being With course session are attempts to describe and facilitate the work of the Spirit. Two foundational principles of the course are:

- the form of the course should match its content;
- the group already has everything it needs, because the Holy Spirit has been working in each participant's life since it began.

The second is obviously an understanding of the doctrine of the Holy Spirit; but the first is really an understanding of the doctrine of the incarnation. Because what is Jesus if not God's commitment to make the form of divine love match its content – to be the embodiment of God's desire never to be except to be with us in Christ? And is not that the tragedy of the church throughout the ages – that its form, wayward, wilful and wild, has so seldom matched its content, the risen Christ met in word and sacrament? The church brings adults to faith through the power of the Spirit ostensibly for their own good; but just as significantly, so they may flood the church with an overwhelming desire and urgent plea that the church's form should match its content. This course gives them the experience to know that it can be true.

2

Method

Recruitment

The first Being With group was announced with a notice at the end of a couple of Christmas Eve carol services. Once you've set a date for the start of a course it's good to find outlets at events or through media where there's a mixed engagement of church regulars, newcomers and outsiders, beginning up to three months ahead of the start date. Every context will vary in relation to use of social media, hard-copy posters, spoken announcements and personal invitations; whether this is an established course that takes place each autumn and spring, or whenever a critical mass of people arises; and whether it is led by church leaders or by lay people.

A suitable spoken announcement might go as follows: 'If you're looking for an opportunity to discover more about Christianity – or take another look, having been away for a while – you may like to join a group starting in a couple of weeks called Being With, which offers a chance to explore what Christianity's really about over ten weeks in a respectful and thoughtful setting. You don't need any prior knowledge, just your life-experience to this point. You can find details in …' This tells people three things about the course: it's serious, and going to take you seriously; it doesn't go on for ever; and it's not going to force anything on you. If everyone who comes to the carol service (or equivalent) finds a card on their chair or pew that can be easily filled in and returned, perhaps also including an appropriate email address, so much the better.

Cold announcements offer maximum choice to the potential participant, but they are nothing like as effective or appreciated as personal invitations. The latter shows real consideration to the person in question, and a genuine judgement that this might be a good fit for them. There's no coercion – but it becomes much harder to say no. One way to tell if a course is catching on is to sense that those who haven't done the course are envious of those who have. If and when that happens, it's probably appropriate to run courses also for those who are church regulars. What works less well is mixing the two groups together. It's too easy for the grey squirrels (the regulars) to chase out the red squirrels (the newcomers).

Leadership

It goes without saying that identifying the right host and storyteller is highly significant. They need to understand their roles; stay in role; and not try to do each other's roles. (That doesn't mean they couldn't change role in another course, or even another session of the same course.)

Hosts need to have or develop the disposition to be more interested in other people's views and comments than in their own. The appropriate state of mind is like a counsellor or a person seeing for the first time a loved one who's been out of touch for a long time and has a lot to tell. There's no need for icebreakers. The host needs to be confident that the participants have joined because they genuinely want to explore Christianity: it doesn't need to be sold to them; they simply have to be given time and space and vocabulary to explore it. The group will go well if the two leaders do their job, and the participants are given the opportunity to develop trust in one another and themselves.

Being a host does involve being dogmatic about certain things, including the following.

- No one gets to comment on what another participant has said – not to express sympathy, say something similar happened to me, or suggest a solution. When online, that includes the chat function: the chat function is not to be used as an alternative, less accountable form of conversation. The host can say in the first session (and repeat if

METHOD

newcomers miss the first session): 'Let's really listen to each other and respect what each other shares. We don't need to comment on what people say. And we do our best not to share elsewhere anything personal that's been said here.'

- Wonderings are not questions. They do not have right answers. They are invitations to reflect and share. It is not a competition.
- Everyone has to contribute to the welcome period, and respond to the question, 'What's been the heart of your week?' or equivalent. If a person arrives late – even very late – the conversation pauses once the person speaking has completed their contribution, and the late arrival responds to the welcome question. The only exception is if the person arrives during the talk, in which case they answer the welcome question as soon as the talk is completed.
- No one is obliged to contribute to the wondering period or the reflection period. It's fine to listen and ponder. There may be very good reasons why a person isn't sharing on a particular topic or at a particular stage of the course. If it looks like a person really wants to speak, for example, someone else keeps getting in first, then the host may explicitly ask them if they want to say something; otherwise the responsibility is theirs.
- Silence is not a problem. If participants are slow to respond, or there's a lull after the first couple of responses, yet the host feels there's more to come, it's fine to leave a period of silence or to repeat the wondering.
- Try to avoid the host or storyteller speaking straight after the other at any stage, especially in the wondering and reflection periods. It can seem like ganging up, particularly if they're both saying something in tension with the previous contribution from a participant. It may also be a sign that one or other is stepping out of role – that is, enjoying themselves so much that they forget their main job is to give space and permission for the participants to make their own discoveries.
- Be aware of the safeguarding policy under which you operate, especially if you feel a disclosure has been made.
- If a participant is especially distressed the host may make contact after the session and if appropriate signpost to support services beyond the group.

BEING WITH: APPROACH

- Each session finishes on time. This is part of the building of unspoken trust with the group. If you prove trustworthy and reliable in small things, the participants will begin to trust you with bigger things.

Storytellers need to be excited about the content of the talks they are going to give, and eager to find connections with the contributions of the group in the first two parts of the session, so as to integrate some elements as examples within the talk. The talk should take six to eight minutes, so the shorter the talk, the more opportunity there is to integrate examples. Around four or five examples is about right. To saturate the talk can make it indigestible. Storytellers need to have the humility to recognize that they are the only person who gets to talk uninterrupted for such a long period, so it's appropriate for them to exercise a certain reticence earlier, by, for example, not responding to all the wonderings, even if they may have perfect responses to each one. It's not necessary to 'know the answer' (no one's certain, for example, when the Bible was written or when its different books were assembled into one combination of Old and New Testaments). More important is to listen to what the question is really asking and be able to suggest an attitude of mind and perhaps a suitable person or author who might be worth investigating to find a fuller answer.

In the event of a person becoming distressed during the session, for example in the course of disclosing a sensitive story, it may be necessary to provide immediate care for that person, perhaps if they withdraw from the room or drop off the online call.

It's important the host and storyteller work together, having a meeting before the session to address any thoughts, concerns or issues from the previous week, and a meeting after the session to discuss anything that came up or offer feedback on the roles taken.

METHOD

Communication

It would be normal for participants to submit an email address when subscribing for the course. They might then expect a blind-copied email inviting them to the first session and suggesting they keep free the proposed dates and times for the nine sessions to follow. That message might go as follows:

> I'm delighted you've signed up for our Being With course, beginning on … at … The sessions last 90 minutes. Each one includes a welcome, a time of conversation known as wondering, a talk, and some discussion. If you have any questions before starting the course, do reply to this message or call me on … Please let me know if you can't come on [Thursday]. Thank you for being part of this course. I hope you'll really enjoy it. Best wishes …

Once you've had the first session, it's best to get into a pattern of a weekly message to all participants. That message can simply say how much you've appreciated people joining in the course so far, and relay the wonderings for the next session, so people can think about them ahead of time if they'd like to.

By the time you get to the eighth session, you need to have worked out what you're offering to participants when they've finished the course. It's not as simple as saying, 'You're now all set – off you go.' Whether you plan to continue with the same group doing a different course, invite group members to join other existing groups, or promise to let them know when subsequent courses begin, you need to be talking about this with two or three sessions still to go. A course run poorly can do damage – but a course run very well that ends badly can do just as much damage. It's quite normal that different members of the group will have different views about whether or not they want the group to stay together – so it's seldom as simple as letting the group decide. It's also unfair on the host and storyteller to ask them to take up an open-ended commitment to the group from the start.

BEING WITH: APPROACH

In-the-room and Online

Being With was devised in the autumn of 2019 as an in-the-room course and began as such in January 2020; but halfway through the first course it became an online experience. Since late 2022 it has reverted to being a largely in-the-room course, but many contexts find online helpful. Online offers some real advantages, including the following:

- Some participants seem quicker to share more deeply when in the comfort of their own homes and when they don't have to walk out of the door with those they've been speaking to.
- As with other online conference-room experiences, there's a much more efficient use of time: no travel, no small talk, no getting up to let people in, no getting lost en route to the first meeting, no being unavailable if you're out of town.
- The storyteller can simply read out the talk in a way that seems perfectly natural, rather than having to memorize it and risk leaving parts out, or fumbling with sheets of paper or an electronic device.
- The host can share the wonderings in the chat, rather than having to hand out sheets or read out the wonderings several times.
- Participants can see each other's names and thus refer to each other by name all the time.
- The course can include participants who live a long way away or even in a different country or time zone.

There are also advantages to in-the-room meetings, including the following.

- There remains an abiding feeling that if you've only known a person on an online conference platform, you haven't really met them, however deep your conversations have gone.
- The ability to sense an inhaling of breath or shift in the chair is easier in the room – aiding the host to hold the silence and space for participants as they share and everyone to pick up the level of emotion in various responses.

- There remains an expectation that participating in the group will lead to joining the congregation at the church, and this has a significant in-the-room dimension in almost all cases – so the threshold needs to be crossed eventually.
- If participants want to build friendships by meeting with one another outside the group time, it's most natural for them to do so before or after one of the in-the-room sessions.

It's worth considering a mixture of online and in-person before assuming a course will be entirely one track or the other.

Beginning

Beginning refers to how you begin the whole course and how you begin each session. As for the whole course, if you're on an online platform, the host will want to be online ten minutes before the official start time. It's not wise to do a last-minute check-in with the storyteller on the same call around this time, since it's likely to be interrupted by an eager early-arriving participant. The host can then be precisely that – the principal welcomer. It's good to stay in role from the very beginning – that is, for the host to do the large majority of the welcoming, to establish from the start to whom the group may look for timekeeping, rule-monitoring and tone-setting. The host can also model the subtle ways in which this course is different from other experiences participants might have had (and might be fearing having again): there are no direct personal questions ('Where are you, Ruth?' – there's no need to put Ruth on the spot; we don't need to know that yet, and she may not want to say), no 'warm-up' icebreakers (this isn't a work team offsite bonding exercise), and no patter (we're not selling people anything or getting people in a good mood).

During the assimilation period (that is, when some members of the group have joined but not all) the host is modelling relaxed, appreciative hospitality. 'Hi, David, great to see you, thanks for joining tonight, this is Julie, Louis, Susie and Alex. We've been talking about our names

BEING WITH: APPROACH

– I was just saying to Louis his name sounds French, but he was saying he's actually Scottish.' Names are a good subject, because they reinforce the process of learning each other's names. It's highly possible not all who signed up will actually appear, so it's good to start soon after the appointed time to model that it's important to show up punctually.

At the first session it's important to set rules and expectations, so the host may say something like this.

> It's great to see everyone at this first session of our Being With course. This is for anyone who wants to explore Christianity for the first time or have another look after a period away. We always do the same four things. We start with me asking, 'What's the heart of your week?' – although we actually have a different question for this first session. Then we do the wonderings. Wonderings are invitations to remember, imagine and discover. They're not questions with a right or wrong answer. We ask everyone to respond to the question at the start, but for the wonderings you say as much or as little as you like. Then X will give a short talk. Then for the last part we reflect and say what we think, and ask questions. The session lasts 90 minutes, so we'll finish at xxx. When people share things it's important to respect what people say. That means we listen gently and don't come in with our solutions or suggestions, even in the chat. It also means we don't talk to other people about something personal that's been shared. OK – we're ready to go. Here's the opening question: 'Tell us a bit about what made you want to come on this course.'

Note that the 'first question' isn't in fact a question. The words, 'Please do treat this time as sacred' can affirm the importance of the session without explicitly demanding confidentiality.

It's very important for everyone to speak in this welcome period – and the 'question' is a helpful prompt for doing so. If a person arrives late, in any session, conversation is paused (except for the talk) to ask them the welcome question. There's always a possibility they've had a bereavement or similarly life-changing event since the last session, and it would be terrible for them not to have a space to communicate that.

METHOD

So making such a space is high priority. 'What's been the heart of your week?' is designed, like almost everything in the course, to be accessed at any level; it may be a momentous event – but it may be a mundane moment that sums up a monotonous few days. The point is the question itself gets participants into gear for what's going to follow: they're going to be invited to perceive the significance in otherwise transient events; begin to examine their lives for the work of the Holy Spirit; and sift out the poignant from the formless mass of memory. This is the beginning of the participants being with themselves by noticing the things that are significant for them in the last week. It's an opportunity to practise presence and attention with themselves towards themselves. So, after 15 minutes of welcome and sharing, the group has (re)formed, and is ready for what's coming.

The session takes a full 90 minutes, so if you're meeting in-the-room, you may wish to allow a little extra time for people arriving, leaving, using the bathroom and taking refreshments.

Wondering

Much has already been said about wondering, so just a few further remarks here. It's important the host truly enjoys the wondering. The first wondering should be read out with genuine fascination and expectancy – not as a performance to entertain, but as if a friend had just returned from Samarkand, and you said, 'Tell me all about it' with real interest. There's no need to pick on people – unless you think they meant to speak but someone else got in first; the host establishes trust when people know they don't need to speak until they're ready. Silence is your friend; it's not a radio show where you need to fill the space with noise; if people are thinking deeply, it's working. In a lull it's no bad thing simply to read out the wondering again. If you're online, you can suggest people indicate they're ready to share simply by unmuting.

It's not essential to get through all the wonderings. You may notice the time, and if you're over 50 minutes in you may feel you want to move on to the talk. You'll know your group. Some groups want to know things and ask things and like a good 25 minutes of reflection time at the end. Others adore the wondering and are quite happy to have just 15–20 minutes reflection. If the host is familiar with the talk, it'll be easier to work out which of the wonderings to leave out if time is short. You can still read the wonderings out and suggest people hold them as they listen to the story.

The wondering can require a good deal of restraint on the part of the host and storyteller. It may be that the storyteller has a perfect response that makes an apt contribution to the conversation: but if there have already been a good number of responses to that wondering, it may be best to hold back. By contrast, if the first couple of responses to a wondering seem to have slightly misunderstood what the wondering was really getting at, it may be helpful for the host or storyteller to interject a contribution that's on message, even if it isn't especially interesting or profound. Most of the leadership in this section is modelling appropriate engagement.

Trust the Group, Trust the Method

Most of the mistakes hosts and storytellers make arise out of anxiety. It may be reassuring to know that before bringing this material to publication many groups have been run, many colleagues have been trained to run groups, and most of those trained have been people the trainers hadn't previously known. Eventually we have reached a point of confidence that this material, handled in the right way, really does have a remarkably high success rate in achieving what it sets out to do.

'Trust the group' is an old adage of this kind of work. Put theologically, God gives those seeking to share faith everything they need to do so; and the most dynamic but often under-used part of that 'everything' is the participants themselves. These people aren't demons sent to undermine or destroy the group, they're angels sent with disarming messages, and the leaders should expect themselves to be moved, charmed and inspired by what the participants say. The reason for the rules is largely to prevent the leaders' anxiety preventing the work the Spirit is doing bubbling up

METHOD

to the surface. It's anxiety that makes leaders try to chivvy the group along, fill silences with inanities or jump on people when they're not ready.

'Trust the method' is perhaps a more surprising thing to say about a course that seems so confident that people's own ways of doing things are valid and important. But, as this guide should by now have demonstrated, every tiny detail of the course has been organized this way for a reason, and if you follow the suggestions made here it should give the right balance of structure and freedom to build trust and enable the participants to flourish. Another feature of trusting the method is a conviction about how people come to faith. The course takes the view that this isn't simply by transferring information via a talk to participants as if their minds were blank slates. The growing sense, cultivated by the wonderings, that the Holy Spirit has already been working in their lives, is often just as significant.

Forming, Growing and Ending

Much has already been said about the first session. It's usually no problem to assimilate new members in the second and third sessions; it becomes harder after that, for the good reason that the group has started to develop trust, and it's quite possible participants have made significant disclosures about very personal things they're not looking to repeat but want the group to remember.

It may be that members of the group find it difficult to keep the 'rules', for example in an online group where they use the chat to comment on one another's contributions. In such a case, rather than risk humiliating people by reacting immediately, it's more satisfactory to reassert some of the initial instructions at the start of the next session. The presence of a new member or two makes this necessary anyway, and avoids the impression that anyone is being highlighted for criticism.

During the eighth session it's time to start naming the fact that the group will come to an end. The host may offer suggestions about how to continue in faith – joining the congregation, perhaps a subsequent Being

With course, or maybe the same group continuing in a second course. While some people find separation very difficult, especially when trust has been profound, the default is to end after the tenth session – because most people are not looking to make an open-ended commitment.

In the final session it's perfectly appropriate to take the last ten minutes to evaluate. For example, 'I wonder what part of the course you liked the best ... I wonder what was the most important part ... I wonder what was the most difficult part.' This can provide invaluable material for improving subsequent courses, as well as providing a healthy closing activity.

Week 11

We tend to refer to what happens after the group has finished as Week 11. There are a number of directions participants can go after finishing the Being With course.

Giving space for the members of the group to decide the direction they would like to take this is important. Pushing the responsibility to them, this could include communicating with each other outside the group meeting or deciding a direction together as a group. This is key if Being With is to become part of the rhythm of your church life with multiple groups per year or over a few years. You will also be able to see the natural leaders emerge and those that could become the host and storyteller next time.

Some will find their way into the life of a congregation – ideally the congregation running the course. It's much easier to join a congregation if you already know some faces there, and if you're not the only newbie – and having participated in a course, this should be the case. People have diverse reactions to feeling their way into a new community: many are shy, reluctant to risk being in a room where they don't know anyone, will only volunteer if personally asked, and remain self-conscious for a long time. A congregation running a Being With course for those beyond its number needs to plan for what a good outcome might look like – and that will most probably mean newcomers appearing. If that isn't your congregation's regular experience, and there aren't systems in place, you

METHOD

might want to anticipate ways to make new faces welcome and expedite a sense of belonging.

Perhaps the most common reaction from participants as they complete the Being With course is, 'Can we do another one?' In many ways this is a very good thing. The bonds made may be remarkably deep – it's common for people to say, 'You know things about me I've never shared with my spouse.' If this has indeed been an encounter with the Holy Spirit – an experience of being with one another that has disclosed what it feels like to be with God – then it's understandable and appropriate that people wouldn't want it to stop. The simplest response is to turn to the volume *Being With: Courses for Living* and proceed with one of those. In that book is Being With Church, which is intended as an adult baptism and/or confirmation course, and other courses on specific areas such as Being With Child and Being With the End of Life.

However, before hastening into a follow-on course, you might want to ask a number of questions. Does this group, united as it may feel, actually represent diverse needs and callings? Some members may be new and enthusiastic, and Being With Church might be right for them. Some may be more established but looking for more exposure to the details of the faith – so might look at Being With the Bible. Others might be interested in a particular issue facing them or the world, and might want to consider Being With Creation or Being With the Other. But there may well be some who've latched on to the method and structure of the course and in whom you see gifts that might make you think they'd be a good fit to train as a host or storyteller. Leaders don't necessarily need to be longstanding Christians – those new or newly returning can bring insight and energy and be a perfect fit, especially if they're paired with a more experienced co-leader. Some within the group may simply view this as a lovely group from which they have learnt a great deal about faith, themselves and others and they just want to continue to meet at a relational level.

A subtler question, particularly for a participant who's joined more than one course, is, 'Might this person be "hiding" in the group as an alternative to joining a congregation more broadly?' There could be many reasons for this, but it's a good question to ponder before simply funnelling them into another group. All groups have to come to an

BEING WITH: APPROACH

end sometime, lest they develop habits of belonging that can become unhealthy and constricting. It's a matter of careful discernment about how to handle such timing, and in almost every case it needs to be a mutual decision rather than one arbitrarily imposed; the discomfort and hurt of a group ending badly can dismantle all the good done by the group having gone well. Of course, there's nothing to stop members of the group meeting with each other informally or socially thereafter – they have each other's contact numbers.

It's often the case that, however positive an experience the group has been, a participant chooses not to pursue life in a congregation or contact with the group thereafter. It's foundational to the Being With ethos that there is no prescribed outcome to the course, so this result shouldn't be seen as a failure of the group, the leaders, the course materials or the participant. The vital thing is that the individual is nurtured and cherished, not least so that should they have a future experience of church they at least have a positive grounding to look back on. It may simply not be the right time, due to work, domestic or other life circumstances; or there may be something about the dynamic in the group itself or in relation to one of the other participants that made things uncomfortable. It may be possible for one of the leaders to seek some kind of a debrief, but if that isn't welcomed, the participant's signal should be respected. As always, our means and our ends need to be identical; this is never about putting pressure on people to do or say something they're not ready or confident to say.

3

Formation

There are four dimensions to getting involved with the Being With course – as a member, host, storyteller and trainer – and it's worth pausing to reflect on the gifts, experience, skills and passions involved in each. Gifts are qualities that you're born with, which you seek to put to use, sometime needing others' encouragement to do so. Experience is the accumulated sum of the events of your life, your relationships, your successes and failures, joys and sorrows, and reflection on each, together with your knowledge of yourself and your world, distilled by reflection, distance and time. Skills are things you cultivate through practice and by copying an expert and get better at. Passions are things you care about with enough intensity that you act on them and pursue a close interest in them.

Becoming a Member

At first glance we might say there are no gifts, skills or passions required to become a member of a group: you simply need to respond to a personal or general invitation and show up at the first meeting, in-the-room or on zoom. But quickly it becomes apparent that we do have certain expectations of group members, and it's important to be aware of what those are.

We assume members have *gifts* and that they are willing to put those gifts to work. Many of those gifts are commonplace – the ability to listen, for example. Others are more distinctive, like the ability to sing, or to run fast – and these may well emerge in the conversations in the group.

BEING WITH: APPROACH

The course assumes that the sharing of *experience*, and its distillation into wisdom, is crucial to being ready to be with God and becomes a vital aspect of encountering God. Being willing to share isn't essential, but being glad to join in appreciating as others share is, as is being prepared to hold with respect the depth of that trust.

No one is expected to display *skills*. In particular, no assumption is made that a member has prior experience of church, knowledge of the Bible, understanding of Christian convictions, ability to remember other people's names, facility in sharing, or ability to remember what others have said. One of the advantages of the group meeting on an online platform is that it's much easier to learn names when they're written on the box in which a person's face appears.

Passions are things you care enough about to shape your life around. The assumption of the course is that God's passion is us; the question of the course is whether God will become ours. It's almost inevitable that this will come to involve some kind of evaluation of the passions of the various members. It's not expected that participants share all their passions and the stories of how they came by them. But it is vital that each respect and cherish the stories shared by others.

Becoming a Host

The point of being a host is to make it look simple. But it's based on the formation of character, careful preparation and rigorous adherence to certain principles – all of which should, with practice, come easily enough to make it look simple.

Formation of character begins with how you feel about the group. If you sincerely believe that the Holy Spirit has been working in the lives of the participants since their lives began, then you approach the sessions looking forward to hearing how the Holy Spirit has been at work – and you concentrate on creating the kind of environment where people will be most comfortable sharing their experience. That means eradicating from your imagination any desire to be the centre of attention, to be thought funny, to be a live wire that gets the party going, or to be the clever one who knows all the answers and has seen it all before. It means being comfortable with silence, because the Spirit is working just as much in the time participants are formulating their thoughts and finding confidence to speak. It means being prepared yourself to share deeply, in order to model to participants that honesty and trust are the watchwords of the group.

Character formation centrally means faith – faith that the Spirit is at work, even if you're not sure how, that there doesn't have to be a predetermined outcome, that a person voicing anger or disappointment isn't going to undermine the process, that something intimate doesn't have to be scary or something personal inappropriate. On the contrary, the skill of improvisation, which the host will develop, is about trusting that the contributions of the participants will be the substance around which the message of the talk finds concrete example.

However simple the group sessions may look and feel, the host's character and preparation are what make them so. The host assembles the names and contact details of the participants, makes sure they have a welcoming message explaining what the group is going to be like, after the first session sends out the wonderings a few days ahead of the subsequent sessions, and logs on to the online platform a few minutes ahead of the others. It's the host who begins to imagine what a follow-up group might entail for the participants either together or individually, and who has already got in mind a few alternatives for each participant or for the group as a whole. The host thinks carefully about each group member ahead of the session, recalls if they referred to a major life event in the previous session that's happened between sessions and needs enquiring about, notes if they had a question there wasn't time to cover in the last session, and is aware if any participant misses a session that this might be for a significant reason.

The group stands or falls on the host's ability to keep discipline and offer clear but simple guidance to participants. Some things only need saying once: 'People may share quite deeply so everyone needs to respect that in the way they talk about this group elsewhere.' Some things probably need saying more than once: 'A reminder that we simply hear and value what we've each said during the wondering time, but we don't

BEING WITH: APPROACH

comment on it or use the chat bar to suggest solutions or make comparisons.' Some things are about tone of voice and economy of words: if a participant has said something very personal or described something painful, the simple and habitual 'Thank you' or 'Thank you for sharing' says all that needs to be said, provided it's said sincerely and tenderly. Some things can't be anticipated: in particular the discussion time at the end of each session often involves participants asking whether their point or query is appropriate and needing reassurance that there are few things too scary to say and the time to ask the burning question is now.

One key point for vigilance is the host's way of relating to the storyteller. It's usually best to develop a good understanding before the first session and to check in between sessions, giving each other feedback and comparing notes on things people have said and anything that could have been handled differently, especially comments that felt uncomfortable enough to need addressing in the next session. If there's tension between the host and storyteller, that needs to be addressed outside the room. But it's perhaps more likely that the host and storyteller will get on very well and enjoy the experience of partnering in offering the course. In that case the danger is that the dynamic between the two takes over the experience of running the group. One good way to prevent this is for them to avoid speaking immediately after one another – whether in the welcome, the wondering time or the discussion. That avoids participants experiencing feeling there's an overwhelming party line that's being presented too forcefully. It also limits the degree to which the group can become a conversation between the leaders to which the participants are just witnesses. It's fine for the host to ask a genuine question of the storyteller during the discussion time – particularly if the question articulates something brewing in the group. But it's less good for the storyteller to offer an answer to a participant's question and the host then to follow up with a similar answer (which may feel overwhelming) or a different answer (which may well be confusing).

FORMATION

Becoming a Storyteller

For most leaders, the idea of becoming a host will be a challenge, but a challenge they feel they can readily accept. More will be daunted by the role of storyteller, even though the script is provided and their engagement in the first 55 minutes or so of each session is not unduly demanding. What is required to be a storyteller?

The storyteller needs to have the character formation, preparation and discipline of the host, even if not acting as the host. This is because the host doesn't always get it right, and the storyteller can gently step in and redirect the conversation. For example, the host may rush on to the wonderings having overlooked one participant in asking the group to answer the opening question, 'What's been the heart of your week?' – in which case the storyteller can simply say, 'I'm not sure we've asked George the heart of his week', or if online send a note to the host in the chat. Likewise the host may forget to ask a latecomer the heart of their week if they arrive amid the wonderings, and the storyteller can prompt the host appropriately.

The most significant role of the storyteller is to listen to the participants' contributions to the wonderings so intently as to be able to integrate some of the responses into the talk. Be careful of the subtle messages you may give in how this is done. For example, if all the illustrations are from the same participant, you'll be saying that participant's contributions are more important (or more important to you) than the other participants'. If you cite an example from the host, you could be taken to be suggesting the host has given the 'right' kind of response. It's fine to make only a couple of such connections: it's not necessary to saturate the talk with them. But they must be made succinctly and in a way that respects the spirit in which they were offered. Because the wonderings have only just been shared, a simple citation is usually plenty – 'As with Brian's dad', 'Like Doreen was saying about her painting class.' Often the example is so recent and vivid you don't even need to give the name of the contributor – and the subtlety makes the insertion even more satisfying.

Most storytellers will be principally concerned about the discussion time, because it's unstructured and because being the storyteller may set them up to be an expert they don't feel themselves truly to be. The secret to handling this is not to get yourself a PhD in theology overnight. It's to be yourself – but also to keep to the character formation and principles assumed by the course. The talk is not your talk – it's come with the course – and while explicitly stating significant disagreement with it may not be helpful, neither is it your duty to defend it against all assailants.

For example, in the first session it would be quite normal in the discussion time for a participant to say, 'Are we always expected to forgive? Aren't there some things you just can't forgive?' The storyteller could say a number of things. One might be, 'I think forgiveness is really difficult in some situations. Maybe forgiveness is always difficult.' Another could be, 'I wonder if anyone would like to talk about an occasion when it was hard to forgive.' Or a third could be, 'When Jesus was on the cross he said, "Father, forgive them." Perhaps that was an indication he himself was finding it hard to forgive so he asked the Father to do it for him.' The first response is neutral, just keeping the ball in play. The second is a move to go deeper, inviting participants to explore the problem rather than to solve it. The third offers a significant theological insight, but again doesn't close the discussion down or offer a reply in defence of the talk – it still invites further reflection. All three are appropriate.

The host and storyteller want to affirm the asset-based convictions of the course – that the group has within it sufficient experience of the Holy Spirit and understanding of who God is in Christ to be sufficient to be with one another and with God. But if a question arises that really does have a yes/no answer ('Doesn't Jesus say somewhere that some things can't be forgiven?'), and neither the host nor storyteller can make a response in the terms the participant requires, it's fine to say, 'I'll have to investigate that one and maybe we can return to it next time.' The crucial point for the formation of the storyteller is that the discussion time is not a press conference, and the storyteller is not a beleaguered politician trying to wriggle out of admitting the truth. Instead, it's a gift of time with each other to explore further and probe more deeply into the argument made in the talk and the issues raised by the wonderings. Constructive feedback in a debrief with the host afterwards is perhaps the best way to learn: 'I wondered if you were a little defensive in that question about how the Bible came to be written'; 'I thought what you said about how you've changed your mind about how to pray for a person with dementia was really honest and helpful.'

Becoming a Trainer

The best way to learn is to teach, and often the experience of training others offers a unique opportunity to reflect on what you're doing and highlight areas where you yourself don't always practise what you uphold. The training covers three areas.

- The first is the immersive experience of being a participant. The storyteller and the host are also participants, and the sessions should be transformative for them too and not just for those who are members of the group. The wonderings are such that multiple different responses surface, and they remain new however many times you conduct the course; and the heart of your week inevitably changes.
- The second is the attentive listening and careful facilitating of the host. This is about recognizing two things: one, you expect the Holy Spirit to be doing wonderful things in the session; two, you assume those things aren't coming primarily through you. Your job is to keep the ball in play, by being comfortable in silence and ensuring everyone's contribution is respected and cherished.
- The third is the storyteller's understanding of what the talk is seeking to achieve and how that can be made even more successful with slight additions to the talk and the right demeanour in the discussion time. Again, most of this is reducing the storyteller's anxiety that they must become the fount of all knowledge and replacing it with a confidence that, the way the course is set up, the important thing is not finding right answers but being one another's companion in the exploration.

Trainers are crucial to the spread of the course. The course really does depend on the formation of its leaders, and training affirms that. Those who are called to become trainers define what the course is and whether

BEING WITH: APPROACH

it can have the maximum effect. To be a trainer is to have confidence in the course and to encourage new hosts and storytellers to trust that, if they perform their respective roles well, glorious things will follow. For further information on this, do visit the Being With website (www.being-with.org).

Part 3
Courses and Commentary

1

The Being With Course

One: Meaning

The present tense doesn't exist. Try to put your finger on it, and whoosh – it's gone. There's no such thing as the present tense.

As soon as we realize this, we become subject to two primal terrors. The first terror is this: you can't stop time. It's out of control. The second terror is this: what we've done can't be undone. However much we try to airbrush the photographs, or fiddle with the timings on the emails, there's no changing what's happened.

And these two terrors – the panic about the past and the fear of the future – together constitute the prison of human existence. There's no genuine living in the present tense, because our lives are dominated by regret and bitterness about the past, and are paralysed by fear and anxiety about the future.

Think about what grieves us. It's what's happened in the past that we can't change, the sequence of events that's led to a kind of prison, to us being in some sense in chains. It's the things we cherish that we dread we can't keep – our youth, our life, the things and the people we love; this very moment right now.

And what does the Christian faith proclaim? Two central convictions. One about the past; one about the future.

The first is about the past. It's forgiveness. Forgiveness doesn't change the things that cause us regret or bitterness. But it releases us from the power of the past. Forgiveness doesn't rewrite history. But it prevents our histories asphyxiating us. Forgiveness transforms our past from an enemy to a friend, from a horror-show of shame to a storehouse of wisdom. In the absence of forgiveness, we're isolated from our past, trying pitifully to bury or destroy the many things that haunt and overshadow and plague and torment us. Forgiveness doesn't change these things but it does change their relationship to us. No longer do they imprison us, pursue us, surround us or stalk us. Now they accompany us, deepen us, teach us, train us. Nothing, in the end, is wasted. That's the work of forgiveness. It's about the transformation of the prison of the past.

Imagine being released from the prison of the past. It's almost beyond our imaginations. It's half of Christianity.

And here's the second conviction. It's about the future. The life everlasting. Everlasting life doesn't take away the unknown element of the future but it takes away the paroxysm of fear that engulfs the cloud of unknowing. Everlasting life doesn't dismantle the reality of death, suffering, bereavement but it offers life beyond death, comfort beyond suffering, companionship beyond separation. In the absence of everlasting life, we're terrified of our future, perpetually trying to secure permanence in the face of change, meaning in the face of waste, distraction in the face of despair. Everlasting life doesn't undermine human endeavour but it does rid it of the last word; evil is real but it won't have the final say; death is coming but it doesn't obliterate the power of God; identity is fragile but that in us that resides in God will be changed into glory.

Imagine for a moment the gift of everlasting life. Feel it slowly dismantle all your worst fears. Let it set you free. Let it give you indescribable joy. It's the other half of Christianity.

The heart of it all is forgiveness and everlasting life. If you have those, nothing can finally hurt you.

Now, for the first time, we can have a present tense – we can experience the present without being tense. That's the most tangible gift of the Christian faith: to enable us to enjoy the 'present' (the gift) of the present tense. The past, what we trust God has done, we call faith. The future, what we believe God will do, we call hope. The present, what God embodies and makes possible, we call love.

Two: Essence

There are two kinds of things: those that abide for ever; and those that last for a limited time. The things that abide for ever we call essence; the things that last for a shorter period we call existence.

We human beings are in the second category. We exist: we think that because we exist, we're the heart of all things. But we forget that existence isn't all there is. We're missing something: something vital. Existence is not the same as essence. Existence is subject to change, decay and death. Essence isn't. Yes, we do exist. But we're not essences: we're not permanent. We're not essential. Take us away and there still is. Our being depends on the existence of others. We crave independence, but independence is an illusion: we never could be independent; and there would be no joy in being so. The longing for independence is the aspiration to be an essence: the secret of happiness is to learn instead to exist.

Why are we here? We exist because the essence of all things, in the depths of its mysteries, brought into being something that was not essential, something … else. We're part of that 'else'. There could have been no existence. There could have been nothing beyond essence. Yet here we are. We're lost in wonder at the transition from eternity to time, from boundlessness to circumscription, from the elusive and immortal to the tangible and fragile. We're bursting with gratitude when we realize that there's nothing whatsoever for which we can claim the credit.

And here, in the depths of wonder, we meet the astonishing claim of the Christian faith. On one starry night, displaced by migration, in a hostile political climate, surrounded by animals, from a young mother living homeless in a strange town, *essence entered existence*. Essence, which we could call by a hundred names but most often call God; essence, which could have remained alone without ever conceiving of existence; essence, which would most straightforwardly have left things as nothing, but, out of utmost grace, initiated existence – that essence made itself part of existence. The Word became flesh. In Jesus, *the essence of all things became part of existence* – subject to change, decay and death, just like us.

Here we discover the answer to perhaps the biggest question of all: why is there something rather than nothing? The answer is because essence, or

God as we usually say, always intended to be our companion, to be with us. That's what the word 'Jesus' represents: God's eternal purpose to be with us, which triggered the whole mystery of existence from beginning to end. Jesus isn't an afterthought that entered existence when essence realized existence was going badly wrong: *Jesus is the whole meaning and purpose for existence in the first place.* Jesus is the reason we exist.

But we haven't yet reached the best bit. Here we come to the most astonishing wonder of all. Jesus is fully human and fully divine – complete existence, utter essence. And through him we realize what God's final purpose always was: *to bring us into essence* – into eternal truth. Jesus is God stretching out a hand and saying, 'Come into the essence of all things to be with me.' Remember the painting of God and Adam on the ceiling of the Sistine Chapel in the Vatican in Rome? God's hand is stretched out in creation. But the final purpose of creation is that God's hand stretches out a second time, in Jesus, and *invites us to become part of the very essence of all things.* What an inexpressible gift.

And so here we are – tiny, pointless, transient specks in the inconceivable enormity of space–time existence. But the personal quality of essence, which we call God, has chosen to enter existence, and become one of us, because of a primordial desire to be with us, in tender, understanding, gentle, humble relationship with us; and that's the reason for existence in the first place. And this being with, which we call Jesus, sets forth a capacity to live in this relationship henceforth, a capacity we call the Holy Spirit; and the ultimate purpose is for God not just to share existence with us but to draw us finally into essence, and dwell with us for ever, even when all existence has passed away. And so every time we form, establish, restore and deepen tender, understanding, gentle, humble relationship with one another, like we're doing right now, we imitate and anticipate the way God seeks to be with us, and glimpse the glory of eternity.

Three: Jesus

The gospel story is, in fact, three interwoven stories:

- The first is Jesus' creation of a new community, based on the hopes of his words and actions. He calls around him 12 companions and commissions them to spread the fire of his message. The companions falter and stumble, out of fear of suffering, lack of imagination, and cold betrayal. But in the resurrection there's promise of a restored community to live his life and share his truth.
- The second is Jesus' mission to the crowd, the teeming mass of the oppressed, who are mentioned over and over again in the story of Jesus' life. This is a ministry of healing, teaching and liberation, through story, announcement and gesture. When Jesus enters Jerusalem on a donkey, the crowd seems to have taken up the cause of liberation. But by Good Friday the people have chosen a terrorist called Barabbas instead.
- The third is Jesus' confrontation with the leaders who held Israel in a stranglehold. One by one Jesus takes on each of the rulers and religious leaders. He dismantles their authority and challenges their control. But eventually the veil is pulled aside, and behind it is revealed the real power in the land, which toys with all other powers – the iron fist of Rome. It's the nails and wood of Roman execution that finally destroy Jesus – only for him to dismantle even Rome's control over life and death.

These three threads – of companions, crowd and authorities – are interwoven in Jesus' story like three strands in a rope. Each finds its climax in the account of Jesus' death. The three stories in the end comprise one story. Jesus' intimacy with his companions, his mission to the crowd and his confrontation with the authorities are all dimensions of his being at the heart of God.

This story is our story. Our story divides into the same three strands as Jesus' story – companionship, issues of inequality, and conflict.

- First, we're part of a group of companions. A Christian is called into relationship with a community. We may already have close family ties. Our call to follow the man from Nazareth may intensify and strengthen these existing relationships, or it may test and challenge them. But either way, we're called to make new, close and accountable relationships with members of Christ's church.
- Second, we're in relationship with those who are oppressed. There are many ways to do this. The relationship that brings about real change is friendship, because to be a friend is to say, 'I am allowing myself to be changed by knowing you.'
- Third, we attend to Jesus' confrontation with the authorities of his day. Jesus is constantly having heated debates with everyone who held the nation in check. The one thing everyone seems to agree on today is that there's plenty wrong with the world. There are only two responses to this – either go and put it right yourself or, if you can't, make life pretty uncomfortable for those who can until they do.

And just as for Jesus' story, these three strands – of accountable community, friendship with those who have their backs to the wall, and challenge to the powerful – all unite in the fundamental story, which is our commissioning by God, our sharing in the mystery of God and our entering the glory of God. Jesus' relationship with God was expressed, discovered and revealed through accountable community, friendship with those who have their backs to the wall and challenge to the powerful. Why should ours be any different?

Our temptation is trying to have the big story, walking with God, without the stories that make up the big story – participation in an accountable community, friendship with those who have their backs to the wall and challenge to the powerful. Our temptation is wanting to have all the benefits of Christian faith without any of the costs. Our temptation is trying to have God without Jesus.

But there's another side of the coin. Getting any one of the strands out of proportion is also a temptation. Look at accountable community. We can easily fall into thinking that's all that matters. We can surround ourselves with people like us. It's the same in regard to friendship with the oppressed. Discipleship isn't a lone quest. When we've discovered the depth of human need, we don't just give in to the temptation of anger or despair, but gather a community of partners and confront those who maintain a pattern of oppression. Again, in relation to challenging the powerful, we mustn't fall into thinking that there's always a simple explanation and the powerful are always to blame. We mustn't assume there's a theory that justifies our anger if such a theory tempts us to neglect our own friendship with the poor and commitment to accountable community.

All of these are temptations to have just part of the gospel – just the community bit, just the oppression bit or just the cage-rattling bit – without the rest. You could say they are temptations to remake Jesus in the image of our own needs and obsessions. They take one of the three strands and ignore the big story. It's the temptation to have Jesus without God.

The gospel leaves us with these three questions.

- Am I a disciple? That is, am I a member of a group of people who hold me to account and challenge me to put my life where my mouth is?
- Am I a friend of those who have their backs to the wall? Have I said to a single person, for whom life is a daily struggle and burden, 'I am allowing myself to be changed by knowing you'?
- Am I confronting oppression? Am I a thorn in the side of those who abuse and manipulate and extort and neglect? Or does the way I spend my money and the lifestyle I unthinkingly adopt simply underwrite and collude in patterns of exploitation and degradation?

These are questions that put feet on the gospel.

Four: Church

There was once a pastor who had an unusual way of finishing the Sunday service. He would bow down to the congregation. He used to say, 'Some clergy bow before the holy table and some bow before the cross. But I'm told that these people are the body of Christ, so I bow before them.' Paul tells us that each member of the church is like an eye or an ear or a hand in the same body. The foot can't say to the hand, 'I don't need you', nor can the eye say to the rest, 'I'm the whole body'. And Paul underlines that the weaker members of the body are vital to its health and welfare. What does Paul mean?

Richard Adams' 1972 novel *Watership Down* tells the story of a dozen rabbits that search for a warren to call home. Each of the communities the rabbits encounter has its own political system. The warren at the beginning of the novel is like a traditional, hierarchical society. The rabbits run away from that warren because they correctly anticipate it's about to be destroyed by humans. A second warren the rabbits meet is run on a totalitarian model. There's one general who keeps all the other rabbits in a state of fear under a military regime. A third community of rabbits seems to resemble a modern decadent society. The rabbits there are somewhat inebriated. Food is plentiful and the living is easy. But the rabbits have lost the ability to find their own food and, more seriously, to tell the truth. They can't bring themselves to acknowledge that they're under the spell of a farmer who feeds them but also snares and kills them one by one. The fourth warren is the one the rabbits found for themselves on Watership Down.

The rabbits discover a great many things through their travels and adventures. The most important thing they discover is that they need each other. One of the rabbits is big and strong; another is quick thinking and imaginative; a third is speedy; a fourth is fiercely loyal; a fifth is a good storyteller. The key rabbit is the smallest and clumsiest, who yet has a sixth sense that anticipates danger – like the destruction of the original warren. What makes this group of rabbits so significant is that they find ways of using the gifts of every member of the party so that they're never short of wisdom and intelligence about what to do next or courage and strength to do what's needed. In other words, the group of rabbits lives and moves and thinks as one body rather than as a dozen separate bodies. There can't be such a thing as an idea or a development that's good for one of the rabbits but not good for the whole body.

This group of rabbits offers us three lessons about what it might mean to be church. First, we can never say we've 'made it'. The rabbits in the story are longing to get to the point where they can say, 'Phew – that's it. We've made it.' Well, there is no such point. The moment never comes. When the dozen refugees meet the easy-living rabbits who live the good life, they can see quite quickly that those inebriated rabbits have lost what it takes to be a community, to tell the truth and ultimately to survive. Jesus' disciples were formed on the way from Galilee to Jerusalem. The church becomes one body as it's bound together on its common journey. It's always a work in progress.

Second, the diversity of the church is a strength, not a weakness. The group of rabbits only survived because it had rabbits with different gifts, different strengths, different visions for what they were doing and where they were going. Paul says there are varieties of gifts but the same Spirit; varieties of ways of serving God but the same Lord.

Once there was a monastery where the monks were constantly at each other's throats, bickering and cursing at one another. One night a mysterious visitor knocked at the monastery door and made a brief but solemn announcement. 'One of you is Jesus Christ.' The atmosphere in the monastery changed overnight. Suddenly each monk treated every other monk with awe and wonder, not sure which one was Jesus but knowing Jesus was among them. They'd learned what it means to be church – to treat one another as we would treat Jesus.

The Bible is made up of 66 books. Each is different, and one or two even seem to contradict one another. If we take it for granted that these 66 books work together to reveal God, why can't we take it for granted that different kinds of churches can also be places where God is made known? We need each other to know God. We cannot say to one another, 'I have no need of you.'

The third thing we learn from the rabbits of *Watership Down* is that being one body isn't just a matter of ignoring differences, allowing tolerance to break out, and dimming the lights to a point where all the rabbits are grey. What saves the rabbits at crucial moments is their willingness and commitment to listen to one another, to hear each other out when they have stories, worries, misgivings or hopes. Out of these curious memories and visions come the gifts that make the group of rabbits so resilient and so adaptable. Paul's picture isn't about bland tolerance. It's about shared direction, wisdom and pain. Being one body is probably more painful than going our separate ways. We spend a lot of our time searching around for vital things that make listening to one another's stories seem like a waste of time. But Paul says to us, 'Your mission is to be one body. Your message is that Christ has made you one body. There isn't anything more important for you to rush off to.' A Christian telling another Christian, 'I have no need of you' is really telling Jesus, 'I have no need of you.'

Five: Bible

The Bible tells a story in five acts. The first act is creation. There was too much love in God for God not to share it. The world isn't the centre of the story; God is. Things do not have to be the way they are – they exist because God chose for them to be. God is the creator, and God is surrounded by creatures. Those creatures don't exist for themselves but have a purpose for God. God made them this way because God wanted one like each of them. Their chief purpose is to glorify and enjoy God for ever. And yet these creatures use their freedom badly. They choose, but have lost the art of making good choices. God pours out just as much love as before but so little is returned; so much creative, playful, joyful energy is wasted. Here's the drama of creation: how God came to turn infinite, divine freedom into a covenant, and how humanity comes to turn finite, created freedom into a prison.

The second act is Israel. God longed to be in true relationship with creation through the part of creation that recognized the divine glory – humankind. God called a man called Abraham, and Abraham followed. The rest of the Old Testament is a love story in which Abraham's descendants strive with God, unable to live with God and unable to live without God. God will not leave them alone: therein lies a promise and a warning. The nation that grew from Abraham exists for God and for the salvation of the nations. Can they find the forms of life that honour its call to be holy? How will God woo or wrest them back when they stray? How far is too far to stray? Will God save the nations another way?

The third act is Jesus. This is the definitive act, at the centre of the drama, in which God's character is revealed; the author enters the drama. In him all the fullness of God was pleased to dwell. There's constantly a human level of encounter, of intimacy and betrayal, of challenge and confrontation. But there's also a cosmic dimension of the magnetism of Jerusalem, the inevitability of his death, the inability of the grave to keep him down. Is God totally vulnerable, or has something been kept back? Will God's people understand, comprehend and follow, or will they seek to overcome, stand over, obliterate and annihilate? Will their rejection of God cause God's rejection of them? If God overcomes death, what will God not do?

Christians are in Act Four, the church. In this act, the church is given all it needs to continue to be Christ's body in the world. It receives the Holy Spirit and is clothed with power and authority. It is given the scripture, made up of the apostolic witness of those who seek to report, while being drawn into, the drama. It's given baptism. It is given the Eucharist, a regular event in which the body of Christ meets the embodied Christ, in a drama of encounter, reconciliation and commission. It is given a host of other practices to form and sustain its life. Will those gifts prove to be enough? Will the church seek solace elsewhere? Will the ways God speaks and acts beyond the church prove more vivid than the ways God's voice is heard and God's deeds are perceived within?

Still to come is Act Five, the end. This is a frightening thing for those who have built up power and resources, but for those who have nothing to lose it's unbounded joy. The timing of the end is not known, but that it will come when God chooses is certain. The drama of that time may yield some shocks – as the secrets of all hearts are revealed. But in God's revelation there will be no shocks, only surprises. For the God who will then be fully revealed will not be different in character from the God who was revealed in Act Three. The face on the cross is the face on the throne.

There are two kinds of mistakes that can easily be made about this five-act drama. The first mistake is to think we're in a one-act play rather than a five-act play. The world – all that has taken God's freedom not yet to believe – thinks it's in a one-act play. In a one-act play, all meanings must be established before the curtain comes down. This life is all there is: heritage has no logical value other than insofar as it contributes to fulfilment here and now. All achievements, all results, all outcomes must be celebrated and resolved before the final whistle. The five-act drama means that Christians are spared such a crisis. They're not called to be effective or successful, but to be faithful. Faithfulness is effectiveness measured against a much longer timescale: since Act Three has happened and Act Five is to follow, Christians can afford to fail, because they trust in Christ's victory and in God's ultimate sovereignty. Their faithful failures point all the more to their faith in their story and its author.

The second mistake is to get the wrong act. This overemphasizes our own role in the drama. If we assume we're in Act One, we place ourselves, rather than God, in the role of creator. There have been no significant events before our appearance in the drama. There's no experience to learn from, no story to join, no drama to enter. This is the desire for independence, to be a self-made individual. No one else's rules have validity: everything must be discovered, named, assessed for ourselves. Similar is the assumption that we are at the end of the story. This is as much the case in the church, thinking it is in Act Five, as in the world, taking itself to be near the end of a one-act play. On the great debating points of church order, people talk as if Jesus and the early church lived an eternity ago, and that they set everything in stone. But what if Jesus lives today, and the church still has thousands or millions of years ahead of it? Perhaps we *are* the early church, still haggling over the details, and rightly so. On nuclear weapons or climate change, people similarly assume that they are near the end of the story. Blowing up the world would indeed be terrible. But the five-act drama proclaims that humanity has already, in Act Three, done the most terrible thing possible by crucifying the Lord of glory.

And a proper understanding of God's sovereignty recognizes that God could well have another world, in all the myriad complexity of this one, all ready and prepared, on hand to replace this one should there ever be a need. Humans are not the creators, nor the finishers, of God's story.

Six: Mission

'With' is the most important word in the Christian faith. Let's explore four models of social engagement.

Working for is where *I* do things and they make *your* life better. Working for is the established model of social engagement. It takes for granted that the way to address disadvantage or distress is for those with skills, knowledge, energy and resources to enhance the situation of those who are struggling. It assumes the advantaged have abundance, which defines them: they should maximize that surplus through education and training; and exercise it through applying their skills broadly. By contrast, the 'needy' are defined by their deficit; if they have capacities, these are seldom noticed or harnessed. Working for identifies problems, focusing on the ones it has the skills and interest to fix. It then moves on to address further such problems, of which the world is never short. It seldom stops to ask why the recipients of such corrective measures are invariably so ungrateful.

Working with is a different model. Like working for, it gains its energy from problem-solving, identifying targets, overcoming obstacles and feeding off the bursts of energy that result. Working for assumes the concentration of power in the expert and the highly skilled. By contrast, working with locates power in coalitions of interest: initially collectives of the like-minded and similarly socially located, but eventually partnerships around common causes, across conventional divides of religion and class. Its stumbling blocks are not the maladies working for identifies; they are pessimism, apathy, timidity, lack of confidence, and discouragement. Working with forms networks and creates a movement where all stakeholders come together and it's possible for everyone to win. Thus it establishes momentum and empowers the dispossessed.

BEING WITH: COURSES AND COMMENTARY

Being with begins by largely rejecting the problem–solution axis that dominates both the previous models. Its main concern is the predicament that has no solution – the scenario that can't be fixed. It sees the vast majority of life, and certainly the most significant moments of life, in these terms: love can't be achieved; death can't be fixed; pregnancy and birth aren't a problem needing a solution. When it comes to social engagement, it believes you can seldom solve people's problems. Doing so disempowers them and reinforces their low social standing. Instead, you must accompany people while they find their own methods, answers, approaches. Meanwhile you can celebrate and enjoy the rest of their identity that's not wrapped up in what you (perhaps ignorantly) judge to be their problem. Like working with, being with starts with people's assets, not their deficits. It seeks never to do for them what they can perfectly well, perhaps with encouragement and support, do for themselves. But most importantly, being with seeks to model the goal of all relationships. It sees problem-solving as a means to a perpetually deferred end. Instead it tries to live that end – enjoying people for their own sake.

Being for is the philosophy that's more concerned with getting the ideas right. It strives to use the right language and have the right attitudes. It wants to ensure products are sustainably sourced and investments ethically funded, people are described in positive ways, and accountable public action is firmly distinguished from private consumer choice. Much of this is good; but in its clamour that Something Must Be Done, it invariably becomes apparent that it's for somebody else to do the doing. The alternative to unwise action becomes not engaged presence but cynical withdrawal: multiple causes are advanced, but their untidy details and complexities are often disdained. In an information-saturated, instantly judging, observer-shaped internet age, it's the default position of perhaps the majority.

Jesus works for us by forgiving sins and opening the gates of everlasting life – achievements concentrated in his suffering, death and resurrection and anticipated in earlier healings and miracles. But Jesus also spends perhaps three years, largely in the north-eastern province of Galilee, where he is calling, forming and empowering followers, formulating a message for them to share, building alliances and confronting

THE BEING WITH COURSE

hostility. One can see the 'saving' as working for, focused on a week in Jerusalem; and the 'organizing' as working with, spread over those years of public ministry. But that still leaves perhaps 30 years in Nazareth, give or take a spell as a baby in Egypt. And here's the question: if Jesus was all about working for, how come he spent around 90 per cent being with (in Nazareth), 9 per cent working with (in Galilee), and only 1 per cent working for (in Jerusalem)? Are those percentages significant, and do they provide a template for Christian mission? Surely Jesus knew what he was doing in the way he spent his time; or do we know better?

We can identify eight dimensions of what being with actually involves. Here are three of the eight.

- One is *mystery*. This rests on distinguishing between a *problem*, which has a generic quality, can be perceived equally well by anybody, can be addressed from the outside and can be solved using skills acquired elsewhere, and a *mystery*, which is unique, can't be fixed or broken down into its constituent parts, is not fully apparent to an outsider and can only be entered, explored and appreciated.
- Another is *delight*. This is the recognition of abundance where conventional engagement is inclined only to see deficit. Delight rejects the template of how things should be and opens itself to surprise and humour and subversion and playfulness. Delight is glad to take time where conventional engagement is overshadowed by urgency. It sees assets where conventional judgement focuses on deficits.
- The seventh dimension, which encapsulates and epitomizes all the previous ones, is *enjoyment*. This rests on a distinction between what we *use*, which runs out and is a means to some further end, and what we *enjoy*, which is of value for its own sake, an end in itself. Being with, simply put, is enjoying people whom the world, having no use for, is inclined to discard.

And so we come to the heart of this course. For by practising being with one another, we discover what it means to be with God.

Seven: Cross

If there's one word that sums up Jesus' story, that word is 'with'. Jesus' ministry, above all else, is about being *with* us, in pain and wonder, in sorrow and in joy, in quiet and in conflict, in death and in life. The Father, the Son and the Holy Spirit are so *with* one another that it seems they are *in* one another. And, to the extent that they are *in* one another, we call God not three but one. God is the perfect equilibrium of three persons so *with* that they are *in*, but *in* in such a way that they are still *with*.

Good Friday is the day we see the very heart of God and the very worst in ourselves. Jesus' last words are 'My God, my God, why have you forsaken me?' At first sight, this is simply the last in a chain of abandonments. Jesus' companions flee, Peter denies, Judas betrays, now God the Father forsakes. It's a litany of desertion. The events leading up to Jesus' crucifixion are a heartless and wholesale dismantling of *with*. Jesus is left *without* all those he worked so hard to be *with* – the disciples, the authorities, the poor – and all of them have not just disappeared but actively deserted or betrayed him. Jesus is still *with* us, but we, at this most precious moment of all, are not *with* him.

But these abandonments are nothing compared to the one that really matters. The cross is a unique event. It's not unique because of how much pain Jesus felt or how much love he'd previously expended. It's unique because the Holy Trinity is the utter presence of unalloyed *with*, and at the moment of Jesus' death, that *with* is, for a brief moment, and for the only instant in eternal history, lost.

With is the very essence of God's being within the life of the Trinity (the relationship of God the Father, Son and Holy Spirit), and the very essence of God's being towards us in Christ. And yet, at this unique moment, that *with* is obscured. Like the clouds coming across the sun, shrouding the earth in shadow, the essence of God, always three persons in perfect relationship, always God's life shaped to be *with* us – that essence is for a moment lost. This is the most poignant and terrifying moment in all history. The two things we think we can know for certain – that God is a Trinity of persons in perfect and eternal relationship, and that God is always present *with* us in Christ through the Spirit – these two certainties are, for a moment, taken away. The universe's deepest realities have become unhinged. The Son is not *with* the Father, even though he desperately wants to be. The Father is not *with* the Son, breaking our whole notion of their eternal presence one with another. This is the most vivid picture of hell we could imagine: not just our being separated from God, but God being separated from God, God being out of God's own reach.

The cross is Jesus' ultimate demonstration of being *with* us – but in the cruellest irony of all time, it's the instant Jesus finds that neither we, nor the Father, are *with* him. Every aspect of being *not-with*, of being *with-out*, clusters together at this agonizing moment. Jesus experiences the reality of human sin, because sin is fundamentally living *without* God. Jesus experiences the depth of suffering, because suffering is more than anything the condition of being *without* comfort. Jesus experiences the horror of death, because death is the word we give to being *without* all things – without breath, without connectedness, without consciousness, without a body. Jesus experiences the biggest alienation of all, the state of being *without* the Father, and thus being not-God – being, for this moment, without the *with* that is the essence of God.

And Jesus' words at this most terrifying moment are these: 'My God, my God, why have you forsaken me?' He's still talking to the Father, even at the moment of naming that the *with* has gone. He's still talking in intimate terms – calling the Father 'My God'. These words come out of the most profound level of trust, the most fathomless depth of *with* and *in*. The most tantalizing thing is that Jesus' last words are a question – a question that doesn't receive an answer. The question should rattle us to our bones.

The question shows us that Jesus has given everything that he is for the cause of being *with* us, for the cause of embracing us within the essence of God's being. He's given so much – even despite our determination to be *without* him. And yet he's given beyond our imagination, because for the sake of our being *with* the Father he has, for this moment, lost his own being *with* the Father. And the Father has longed so much to be *with* us that he has, for this moment, lost his being *with* the Son, which is the essence of his being.

Here we are, at the central moment in history. Jesus, the incarnate Son of God, has to choose between being with the Father or being with us. And he chooses us. At the same time the Father has to choose between letting the Son be with us or keeping the Son to himself. And he chooses to let the Son be with us. Can you believe it? That is the choice on which our eternal destiny depends. That's the epicentre of the Christian faith, and our very definition of love.

These two astonishing discoveries, the Father's losing the Son for us and the Son's losing the Father for us, rattle our bones because they make us wonder, 'Is all then lost?' – not just for us, but even for God. Has the Trinity lost its identity for nothing? If we don't experience a shiver of this greatest of all horrors at this point, then we haven't allowed ourselves truly to enter Good Friday. But this deepest of fears is what will find an answer two days later, when we find that neither sin nor suffering nor death nor alienation has the last word. *With* is restored at Easter, and, on the day of Ascension, *with* has the last word.

Is our alienation from God really so profound that it pushes God to such lengths to reverse and heal it? We don't want to believe it. But here it is, in front of our eyes. That's what the cross is – our cowardice and cruelty confronted by God's wondrous love. Is being *with* us for ever really worth God going to such lengths to secure? Now that is, perhaps, the most awesome question of all. It takes us to the heart of God's identity, and the heart of our own. Can we really believe God thought we were worth it? Are our paltry lives worth the Trinity setting aside the essence of its identity in order that we might be *with* God and incorporated into God's life for ever?

Jesus' cry is one of agony that to reach us he had, for a moment, to let go of his Father. What is our cry? Our cry is one of grief, that we were not *with* him. It's a cry of astonishment, that he was, despite everything, still *with* us. And it's a cry of conviction and commitment, that we will be *with* him henceforth and for evermore.

Eight: Prayer

Here are four parts of a conversation you might have with someone from a different place in society from yourself:

- Tell me about the ways you are rich.
- Tell me about the ways you are poor.
- Let me tell you about the ways I am poor.
- Let me tell you about the ways I am rich.

Maybe the conversation might go something like this. You'd say, 'Tell me about the ways you are rich.' And your friend might say, 'I appreciate the way you see me for what I am and not just for what I'm not. My childhood was difficult, but I feel rich in the variety of people my parents brought into my life. My education wasn't very successful, but I feel rich in the way I learned to read people and look into their hearts. I feel rich in the wonder of the birds and their song and the dawn and its beauty and the pouring rain and its refreshment. I've never had much money, but I have a wealth of friends and somehow there's always been someone who's stepped out of the shadows to help me when I couldn't manage everything myself.'

And then maybe you'd say, 'Tell me about the ways you are poor.' And your friend might say, 'You're probably expecting me to talk about how I can't pay the rent and can't find a job. But the real way I feel poor is when I see a person who's a lot worse off than me and I feel powerless to help them. The real times I feel poor are when I see a newcomer to this country trying to make their way and I can't speak enough of their language to be much use to them. The real times I feel poor are when I think of my daughter who died when she was just two and I was just 19, and I miss her with more sadness than I have in my whole heart.'

And then maybe you'd say, 'May I tell you about the ways I am poor?' And your friend might say, 'I'd never thought of someone like you as poor.' And you might say, 'I felt I had to apologize for being a girl. All my life I've struggled with envy. I've always hated my brother, even though I've never told him, and anyone would think we were the best of friends. I wonder if I've ever trusted anyone enough to show them who I really am. But I'm also rich. I've always had the ability to concentrate. I can listen, or read, or even be silent and pray, for hours. And I can paint. I can paint a watercolour, I can paint a miniature, I can paint a wall, I can paint a face, I can paint anything and make it laugh and dance and spring to life. I share my heart through my paintbrush.'

When the two of you have shared your wealth and your poverty with one another in this way, you may want to leave it there. But you may choose to go a little further.

Your friend may say to you, 'Let me tell you about how you're rich. You're rich because you don't have to spend every waking moment of your day earning money, so you've got time to do beautiful things and walk with people who are in trouble. And let me tell you how you're poor. You're poor because you've never found a way to love your brother. You're poor because you don't have enough people like me around you to tell you the truth about yourself.'

And then, ever so tentatively, you may find the courage to say to your friend, 'You're rich because your laugh is infectious and exciting. You're rich because every child you ever meet loves you. You're rich because you've already been through the worst that life can bring so you live without fear. But you're also poor. You're poor because you're deeply hungry to do something really useful for others but you can't find a way to do it.'

If you have the first kind of interaction, that's called a conversation. But if you have the second kind of interaction, where you talk about each other, that's more than a conversation. That's called a real relationship.

Poverty is a mask we put on a person to cover up their real wealth. And wealth is a disguise we put on a person to hide their profound poverty. Those we call the rich are those in whom we choose to see the wealth but are more reluctant to see the deep poverty. Those we call the poor are those in whom we choose to see the hunger but are slower to see the profound riches. God takes that in each of us that is rich and sees through it to our poverty. And God takes our poverty and sees past it to our deeper riches.

And every day we enact these words before God. We think of our neighbour, in person, society and globe, and we reflect on their wealth – and we consider the wonder of God's universe. And we call that praise. We think of our neighbour in their poverty and all that's wrong in the world, and we call that intercession. We think of ourselves in our poverty and of everything we could have done differently, and we call that confession. We think of ourselves in our riches and all the blessings of our life, and we call that thanksgiving. These are the four parts of prayer. Praise, intercession, confession, thanksgiving. The riches of the world, the poverty of the world, the poverty of ourselves, the riches of ourselves. These are the ways we make that courageous intimate conversation a daily act of renewal.

Have that conversation with someone this week. Make it the time you remember that Christ left his wealth and took on your poverty that he might make you wealthy in the way he is wealthy. Make it the time you discover another's poverty and another's wealth, and redefine your own wealth and your own poverty. Have that sacred conversation with another person this week.

But have that conversation with God every day. For that's what prayer is. Prayer is when we see God's wealth and God's poverty, and bring to God our poverty and wealth, and our neighbour's too. That's a daily conversation, in which our friendships, our lives and our world are being transformed.

Nine: Suffering

Let's imagine a conversation over coffee after church. You say hi. You say, 'We haven't talked for a while. How are you, what's up?' And you catch up on this or that. And then, just as you're finishing, your conversation partner holds your forearm, her tone changes and is more serious, and she says, 'Say a prayer for my dad, will you, he's not himself, the dementia's really kicking in now, and I feel like he's losing his identity inch by unrelenting inch.' And you look into your friend's eyes, and in them you see the cost of what is required to keep going, and of what it has taken just to put that pain into words, and you say, 'I'm sorry. I'm so sorry. This must be such a bewildering time for you. Of course I'll pray for your dad. And I'll pray for you too.'

But then you've made a promise, a promise you have to keep. How exactly do you pray for a person in such a situation? What words can you find to wrap around this kind of long, slow-burning tragedy, in which lives and souls unravel and there's no sign of the dawn?

There are two conventional ways to pray for your friend and her dad. I'm going to call the first way resurrection. It's a call for a miracle. You just say,

'God, by the power with which you raised Jesus from the dead, restore this man in mind and body, make him himself again, and bring my friend the joy of companionship and the hope of a long and fruitful family life together.'

There's a big part of you that wants to pray this prayer. You love your friend. You see how watching her dad disintegrate before her eyes is breaking her heart. You want God to show some compassion, some change, some action. In the back of your head, you maybe have a sense of some Christians, perhaps close to you, who seem to pray for resurrection all the time, and you wonder if you should have more faith and expect God to do amazing things every day. But you've also seen hopes dashed, you've seen Alzheimer's only end one way, and a part of you can't even say the word 'heal' because it seems to be asking for something that just isn't going to happen. That's the prayer of resurrection. You know Christianity's founded on it, and you know it's what your friend most longs for – but sometimes you just find it too hard to say.

But that's not the only kind of prayer. The other conventional kind of prayer is the prayer of incarnation. It's a call for the Holy Spirit to be with your friend and her father. It's a recognition that Jesus was broken, desolate, alone, on the brink of death, and that this is all part of being a human being, all part of the deal you sign on to the day you're born. Our bodies and minds are fragile, frail and sometimes feeble. There's no guarantee life will be easy, comfortable, fun or happy. The prayer of incarnation says,

'God, in Jesus you shared our pain, our foolishness and our sheer bad luck; you took on our flesh with all its needs and clumsiness and weakness. Visit my friend and her father now: give them patience to endure what lies ahead, hope to get through every trying day, and companions to show them your love.'

The irony about this prayer is that the resurrection prayer expects God to do all the work, whereas this prayer stirs us into action ourselves. If we say, 'Send them companions to show them your love', we've got to be wondering if there's anyone better placed to be such a companion than we ourselves. Deep down your friend is well aware that the prospects for her father are pretty bleak. What she's really asking for, when she nervously puts her hand out to clasp your forearm, is, 'Help me trust that I'm not alone in all of this.' Chances are, you can help her with that. But in the midst of it all, you'd hardly be human if you didn't feel powerless and inadequate in the face of all she was going through.

I want to suggest that resurrection and incarnation aren't the only kinds of prayer. I'm sure they're the most common, and in many circumstances they say pretty much all we want or need or ought to say. But there's a third kind of prayer – a prayer of transfiguration:

'God, in your son's transfiguration we see a whole reality within and beneath and beyond what we thought we understood; in their times of bewilderment and confusion, show my friend and her father your glory, that they may find a deeper truth to their lives than they ever knew, make firmer friends than they ever had, discover reasons for living beyond what they'd ever imagined, and be folded into your grace like never before.'

This is a different kind of a prayer. The prayer of resurrection has a certain defiance about it – in the face of what seem to be all the known facts, it calls on God to produce the goods and turn the situation round. It has courage and hope, but there's always that fear that it has a bit of fantasy as well. The prayer of incarnation is honest and unflinching about the present and the future, but you could say it's a little too much swathed in tragedy.

Maybe this is your real prayer for your friend and her father. Maybe this is your real prayer for yourself, in the midst of whatever it is you're wrestling with today. Not so much, 'Fix this and take it off my desk!' Nor even, 'Be with me and share in my struggle, now and always.' But something more like:

'Make this trial and tragedy, this problem and pain, a glimpse of your glory, a window into your world, when I can see your face, sense the mystery in all things and walk with angels and saints. Bring me closer to you in this crisis than I ever have been in calmer times. Make this a moment of truth, and when I cower in fear and feel alone, touch me, raise me and make me alive like never before.'

Ten: Resurrection

Imagine you're in heaven and you're looking back on eternity to select the very best day of them all. We could suggest six finalists and consider their merits. Let's take them in chronological order.

How about the day of creation? It's got fabulous fireworks. It's got exponential imagination. It's the day the inner imagination of God got externalized and turned into tangible form. Do you think the whole history of the universe was contained in embryo on this day, like a tiny egg that contains a person's whole future?

Our second candidate is the day of the exodus. This is the great day when God parted the Red Sea and took the descendants of Abraham, who'd been enslaved in Egypt, to freedom. Everyone was awestruck by the power and purpose of God. Just imagine the collective joy and discovery that nothing was impossible with God. Great day.

Our third candidate is the day of the covenant, when God gave Moses the Ten Commandments and God's commitment to Moses' people crystallized in promises and guarantees and tangible forms of loyalty and love. It was the day that defined what it meant to be God's people and how to live for ever in peace with God and one another. It was the original mountain-top experience.

Then to our fourth candidate. It's Christmas. The day we discover that God loved us so much as to become one like us. God affirmed creation so deeply that, despite our sin, God thought it was worth entering our life, taking on our mantle and inhabiting our existence. God coming at Christmas was the reason for creation. God made the world to be with us in Christ.

But then there's Good Friday. On the day of the exodus God's people saw God's power. On Good Friday we see God's love. Hands that threw stars into space to cruel nails surrendered. What wondrous love. Could any day surpass this?

Well, here's a candidate. What about the Last Day? The last day of all. The day when Christ comes back. The day when everything that's been wrong in all the history of time gets set right, when all who have been downtrodden are seated on thrones, and all who have lost their lives in tragedy find untold joy. The day when evil is finally expunged and sin can plague us no more. The day when everything that creation was meant to be but never quite became is transformed and creation is restored, iridescent, changed from glory into glory and showered in wonder, love and praise. Beat that.

Well, I think we can beat the Last Day.

Early in the morning, depending on which version of the story you read, there was one woman, or three, or two men, who went to a tomb. It's a day that began as one of the saddest-ever days. But before breakfast time it had turned into the Day of Days – not just the greatest day of them all, but the day that contained all the other six. Just see how this day, this holiest, most astonishing and wondrous day, is all the other six days wrapped into one.

It's another creation day because, look, it's Jesus and Mary, a man and a woman in a garden, just like creation, and it's a day of limitless possibility. It's almost literally the first day – the first day of Christianity, of the past released by forgiveness and the future unleashed by eternal life. It's the beginning of everything. It's the Great Day.

And look, it's another exodus. Moses and his people were led out of the slavery of the Egyptians – we this day are set free from evil, sin and death. It's the exodus again, but not just for a small number of people long ago;

this time it's for everyone, for ever. It's the end of the night of suffering and misery and the dawn of the eternal day of glory, hope and joy.

And see how it's another covenant. The first covenant came with smoke and earthquake and fire. This one too came with portents surrounding Christ's death and an earthquake that moved the stone. The first covenant showed Israel how to stay close to God; this one shows everyone that nothing can separate us from the love of God – not even death itself. Whatever we throw at God, however deeply we reject God, however much we seek to bury or destroy God, God will find a way back to us. That's the truest covenant of all.

And look how it's like Christmas all over again, but bigger. Christmas affirms the fleshly, tangible, earthiness of human existence. Easter does so again, but this time after humanity has demonstrated one almighty allergic reaction to the goodness of God. Everything the incarnation proclaims and embodies, the resurrection affirms twice over: God will be with us in Christ, not just out of primordial purpose but even when we have done our absolute darnedest to expunge Christ from our presence. Resurrected life is bodily. The human body has an eternal destiny.

And most obviously, Easter is Good Friday again. Jesus shows his disciples his hands and his side. He is the good shepherd who has laid down his life for his sheep. And now this blessed morning he begins to go around reassembling his flock, starting with Mary Magdalene. Good Friday shows us that God will be with us even if it splits God's heart in two, even if it threatens to sever the inner-Trinitarian relationship of the Father and the Son. Easter shows us that nothing whatsoever can stop God being with us, not just at the most intense moment in history – but for ever.

And then finally Easter is everything the Last Day will be, but in microcosm. Like the Last Day, Easter restores creation. Like the Last Day, Easter vindicates the oppressed, in this case Jesus, and exalts the humble and meek. Like the Last Day, Easter is the enactment of every single one of the Beatitudes. Jesus is the pure in heart. Jesus is the peacemaker. Jesus is the one who hungers and thirsts for righteousness. Jesus is the one who is reviled by all people. And on the day of resurrection, he's happy, he's blessed, he's called God's child, he's laughing.

This day, this wondrous, glorious, blessed, fabulous day – this day is the greatest day in the history of the universe and the story of heaven. This is the perfect seventh day, the day that comprises and epitomizes and embodies and expresses all the other six great days of all time. This is the day in which all the suffering, all the imagination, all the love, all the freedom, all the grief, all the justice, all the hope, all the wonder are combined in a mixing bowl, left behind a huge stone, and like yeast acting on a mixture, burst out, push that stone away because there's so much life there nothing can keep it in, no one can keep it down, no force in heaven or earth can stop it now.

This is the day. This is the great day. This is the glorious day. This is creation, liberation, incarnation and consummation all wrapped into one. This is the day when we stand on the shoulders of God, and say, 'I can see for ever!' This is Easter Day.

2

Commentary on Talks

One: Meaning

The first talk starts with an apparently confrontational claim: 'The present tense doesn't exist.' On closer inspection, it's not such a radical thing to say. The present tense is always in motion and never static. By starting in such an arresting way, the talk seeks to change the default expectation that the participants come with awkward and challenging questions, while the storyteller and host are defending a familiar but flawed gospel. Instead, here, from the very outset, it's the storyteller that's setting out an enormous challenge: that the one thing all participants can be fairly confident about – that they are living in the present tense – is not what it seems.

Having ploughed up the ground of what we usually take for granted, the storyteller then explores the two areas where the participants in most cases come to the course with profound anxieties. This is not an attempt to exacerbate those anxieties, but to name them and embrace them, as something that no longer needs to be secret and suppressed, but can now be acknowledged and transformed. The participants in many – probably most – cases come to the group with a fear and a suspicion. The fear is that if the group members – especially the host and the storyteller – knew who they really were, the thoughts they really had, and in some cases the things they had done, then they'd be thrown out of the group. The suspicion is that the church is a bunch of hypocrites and those joining a course are making themselves vulnerable to being lectured at by people who have no right to think of themselves as better than others.

COMMENTARY ON TALKS

This first talk recognizes those two premonitions but isn't distracted or intimidated by them. It distinguishes between the two dimensions of the past – what has been done to us, which has left hurt and damage, and what we have done, which leaves guilt and regret. Together, these constitute a prison: the prison of the past. It's important to take this part slowly, so listeners can grasp the comprehensiveness of these two legacies. Then, taking a line from the Apostles' Creed, the storyteller explains what Christianity offers: forgiveness. This means the healing of the past. It doesn't mean the storyteller expects participants to forgive everyone who's hurt them there and then, or dismisses their shortcomings and failures as trivial and easily transcended. Instead it's an invitation to the group members to imagine all the damage of the past being lifted off their shoulders and no longer able to inhibit their life and future.

Then the storyteller turns to the future and names our two principal terrors about it: what we know, especially the inevitability of our approaching death, and what we don't know – what may lie ahead of us, especially what may or may not happen after our death. Again, taking a line from the Apostles' Creed, the storyteller introduces the notion of the life everlasting. This takes away the fear of the future. It doesn't explain everything about death and what happens after, but it expresses the conviction that the God who has been with us in life will be with us beyond death.

The talk includes opportunities to digest the wonder of these two gifts and to bask in the grace of the God who gives them.

Then the talk reintroduces the notion of the past, future and present that's been implicit throughout, and comes to a climax by giving each a new name. The past becomes faith – what God has done; the future becomes hope – what God will do; and the present becomes love – what God is doing. The pun – that the word 'present' can mean now but can also mean gift – isn't essential to the argument, but makes a satisfying conclusion. The introduction of faith, hope and love reaffirms the comprehensive nature of this vision: it's all that Christianity brings, rendered in three familiar words – and it's addressing our deepest feelings, of guilt, bitterness and fear.

The overall claim is in sharp contradiction to the way Christianity is often perceived. Many assume Christianity is life-denying, and suggest that without the constraints and prejudices of religion, people could live freely. This talk, without denying the many failures of the institutional church and its representatives, makes the opposite claim: without what Christianity offers us – the healing of our past and the gift of our future – we cannot truly live. It's precisely because God wants us to be fully alive that Christ delivers us from the prison of the past and the fear of the future. Forgiveness and everlasting life are not free-standing gifts as they might be presented in some forms of historic Christianity: they're gifts for a purpose. That purpose is that God might be in full relationship with us. Thus the talk keeps to the theological principle underlying the course: that being with, displayed in the incarnation, is the reason for creation and the nature of eternal life. There is complete continuity between them all – and that continuity is both the message and the method of the course.

The secret of the reflection time that follows this talk is not to feel you have to be the expert about things no one is an expert about. No one knows what follows death: Christianity claims that, after death, the Holy Spirit makes a new, embodied life out of all that in our earthly life turned to God; and that is the claim that this talk presupposes, with a confidence based on the God who raised Jesus from death. But no one can assert expertise about such things. The role of the storyteller and host is to affirm people as they begin to imagine what life would be like if we were free from fear and regret. It's those feelings, rather than intellectual queries about the nature of the afterlife, that prove the most productive. Nonetheless it's vital to accept all contributions and not to quash a conversation, even if it's not headed in the most fruitful direction.

A shorter version of this talk appears as part of the introduction to Samuel Wells, *A Future Bigger than the Past: Catalysing Kingdom Communities*.

Two: Essence

The second talk is ambitious because it seeks to articulate why God created the universe, who Jesus is and what will be our destiny for ever. These are big questions and it's very appropriate for participants to hope the course will address them. The surprise is not that the talk takes these questions very seriously, or that it's so wide-ranging in its scope, but that the answer to all three of these grand questions is the same. The answer lies in God being with us.

God being with us is the answer to who Jesus is: and this answer provides the answer to the other two questions. God created the universe to be with us in Christ, and God will be with us in Christ for ever. The important thing to recognize is the way this differs from conventional notions of who Christ is. The familiar version of the story is that Adam and Eve sin, God calls Abraham, Jacob goes down to Egypt, Moses brings Israel out of slavery, kings build the temple, Israel falls from grace and finds itself in an exile that's only partially ended when it returns from Babylon, and Jesus comes along to restore God's relationship with Israel and transform it into forgiveness and eternal life for the whole world. The problem with this version of the story is that Jesus isn't really the centre of the story. The centre of the story is the achievement of our salvation. It's a human-focused story. By contrast, the story told in this talk is always, all the way through, about Jesus. God chooses never to be except to be with us in Christ. God makes human beings precisely as creatures to be with. (In the traditional version, it's never entirely clear why God creates at all.) It's a God-focused story.

The talk begins by making a distinction between essence, which lasts for ever, and existence, which lasts for a limited time. The key insight is that God is more real than we are – essence is more real than existence. The aim is to decentre participants from a world view that places themselves at the heart of all things, to one that puts God at the heart of all things. It's also to make the point that it's almost impossible to be an atheist. Because 'God' is simply the name for whatever you think it is that lasts for ever. What's radical and interesting about Christianity is not that it believes there's such a thing as God, but that it believes that God is personal and wants to be in relationship with us. The notion of God, in a general way, detached from Jesus, is not an argument Christians have much of a stake in.

Once the talk has decentred humankind and put God at the centre of the story, a bunch of questions arise. The most significant one is: why is there something rather than nothing? The answer to that question reveals the awesome series of consequences dependent on God's purpose to be in relationship with us. One thing is unveiled after another. Essence enters existence; being with is the original purpose of God; and God's final intention is to draw us into essence, and thus to be with us for ever.

The final paragraph begins to make the connections that underpin the whole course. Every time we form or restore relationship, we reflect, imitate or anticipate God's fundamental purpose, which is to be with us – a relationship that needs constantly forming and restoring. It may begin to dawn on some participants that this is why the course is so carefully set up in the way that it is: because the course is designed to enable people to begin relationship – with one another, with the church, and thus with God. From starting on a truly universal scale, the talk ends with very ordinary relationships, whose significance is now elevated on to a cosmic scale.

Because the language of essence and existence sounds bold and grand, some people can initially be put off and feel it's too much – too abstract and remote, too hypothetical and challenging. But the ideas are really very simple, and their power lies partly in the way they address the greatest questions of existence in an uncomplicated and succinct manner. Once people have assimilated the first two talks, they should have a healthy confidence that this Christianity has the breadth and attractive power that they were looking for – but which is too seldom associated with the church.

It's not necessary to dwell on the ways this portrayal of Christ differs from the more familiar account. That will become further apparent in the way the cross is described later in the course. By that stage, participants will have a richer vocabulary of being with to be able to understand the significance of what's being shared. At this stage, it's more helpful to focus on the way this talk concludes, and emphasize that in each act of

COMMENTARY ON TALKS

forming and restoring relationship, we're getting a glimpse of the heart of all things.

This talk is an abbreviated version of the opening words of Samuel Wells, *Walk Humbly: Encouragements for Living, Working, and Being*.

Three: Jesus

In an old-fashioned Introduction to Theology course, the second talk might be described as 'Christology from above', and this third talk as 'Christology from below'. In other words, the second talk takes for granted that Jesus is divine, and seeks to show how his becoming human was crucial in bringing God and us face to face with one another. The third talk takes for granted that he was human, and seeks to show in what respects that humanity is the form in which he displays his full divinity.

It relies on a careful analysis, especially based on Mark's Gospel, of the way the story is constructed around three kinds of relationships Jesus has: with his disciples, with the poor and with the authorities. The talk conveys a good deal of the gospel story, but rather than adopt simple narration it invites the listener to engage critically, thus gaining an insight into the politics of the gospel stories. Just as the first talk points towards the difference Christianity practically makes to being able to be fully alive, so this third talk highlights the difference between the ways Jesus spent his ministry and the way we spend our lives.

The crucial step in grasping the talk is to perceive the people with whom Jesus spent his time as a template for the people with whom we should be spending our time. Rather than choose between church (the 12 disciples) and God's realm (the poor and the controversies with the authorities), the emphasis is on being with both. Everyone is different, so everyone will have their own balance of where they're most inclined to spend their time, and which kinds of encounter they're most likely to avoid. By affirming diversity of response within a comprehensive framework, this argument is designed to offer a holistic vision while nonetheless celebrating difference.

But there's also a lot of challenge in this address. The first two addresses, while very personal, were ones the participants could hold at arm's length. This talk presents two rival temptations: the temptation to have God without Jesus and the temptation to have Jesus without God. Rather than present doctrine as a faraway thing where you can pick and choose the bits that seem amenable and relevant to you, this vividly demonstrates the ethical implications of doctrinal convictions, in the simple and concrete terms of whom your life is shaped around. Adapting an expression of St Oscar Romero, the talk concludes by saying these are ways of putting feet in the gospel.

The overall intention is to take Jesus' ministry more seriously and to gain a richer understanding of the Bible. If the assumption is that Jesus came to die to take away our sins, the details of the gospel story don't matter very much. But if Jesus' life is a template for our lives, the details of the gospel story become tremendously important. Jesus becomes the heart of God laid bare before us, and we're drawn to study the fine details of each parable, encounter, sermon and activity as a clue to disclose how God calls us to live, and who God actually is. It transforms the way we read the Bible.

This talk is adapted and abbreviated from a sermon that was published in Samuel Wells, *Speaking the Truth: Preaching in a Pluralistic Culture*, revised and expanded edition, *Speaking the Truth: Preaching in a Diverse Culture*. The insight about Jesus spending time with three kinds of people comes from Ched Myers, *Binding the Strong Man: A Political Reading of Mark's Story of Jesus*.

Four: Church

The fourth talk makes it clear that what the course is offering isn't head-knowledge or simply an experience limited to feelings: if this is going to be a lasting change of identity and life-direction, we need, early on, to come to some understanding of the church. There are plenty of reasons not to like the church, and some participants in the course will have been bruised by the church and/or its representatives in some way. But in the end what's wrong with the church is that it's made up of flawed individuals just like the participants in the course: pride, envy, greed, lust and sloth are widespread. It is, after all, a hospital for sinners more than a school for saints.

How then may we think of the church in a way that accepts without excuse its many failings yet holds on to the conviction that Jesus really intended it? The approach taken in this talk is designed to combine a sense of the energy generated when a group of people coalesce around a single project with the conviction that God gives the church everything it needs – provided it's prepared to harness all the gifts God sends it. Many are familiar with the words of the anthropologist Margaret Mead: 'Never doubt that a small group of thoughtful, committed citizens can change the world; indeed, it's the only thing that ever has.' This talk gives texture to such a sentiment by demonstrating the way a thriving community puts to work the gifts of all its members.

The point is to create an expectation in participants not only that they are going to be joining a community but that from the outset they can expect to be contributors to that community rather than simply consumers. While the story of *Watership Down* is 50 years old, it's at root a timeless parable; but more than that, it's a political fable in a way few who know the story identify but almost anyone can easily relate to. It makes an apt illustration of Paul's words in Romans 12 and 1 Corinthians 12 about the church as the body of Christ. The analogy enables the talk to draw out three features of church that recognize the church's many shortcomings but offer positive ways for participants to engage in it wholeheartedly: it's a work in progress, its diversity is a strength, not a weakness, and it takes serious effort.

In this last point lies the beginning of a healthy critique of a bland tolerance that tends to thrive in environments that define themselves against what they see as conservative narrowmindedness. 'Live and let live' is not a serious ethic – because it gives you nothing to say when the other person isn't, as you see it, letting live. Some pain isn't just inflicted by malign forces closing down other people's diverse expression, and can't simply be alleviated by expelling or winning round those malign forces: some comes from a community striving to live with different perceptions of the good, and from individuals' unwillingness to stay in a place of tension without flouncing out or seeking to dominate. What the course is offering participants is a promise of life in community that honours and harnesses the gifts of all but doesn't deny the disciplines needed and the disappointments that arise when not all goods can be realized all the time.

The line about the Bible's 66 books is an example, reminiscent of talk three, of how a good deal of factual information can be conveyed while in the midst of offering an analogy about something else. This is absolutely not a Bible-knowledge class, but some useful things can be communicated in the course of explaining, in this case, how diversity works for good. The subtle point is that diversity wasn't invented in the last few decades by enlightened people who realized everyone had a right to be themselves. Diversity was right there when the Bible was put together, when four Gospels were included rather than one, when the New Testament didn't supersede the Old, when a bunch of letters were included in the New Testament whether or not they were written by Paul, and some books, like Esther, Ecclesiastes, Song of Songs or James, were included in the Bible whether or not they were in tension with the thrust of the majority of the books that surrounded them.

Participants may protest that they'd prefer to have Jesus without the church. They may have very good reason to do so. They should not be shouted down. Their views count for much. The reflection time does not need to be unanimous or reach consensus. There's little gained by trying to give participants too rosy a picture of the church. But this session gently asserts that there's no Christianity without it. The talk offers the only reference to baptism in this course. It's something to be developed elsewhere, but it's so integral to the notion of Christian identity that it gets a fleeting mention early on.

The talk began as a sermon that was adapted for a section in Samuel Wells, *A Future that's Bigger than the Past: Catalysing Kingdom Communities*.

Five: Bible

How do you communicate the heart of what the Bible has to tell us, plus some kind of overview, in a digestible form that takes under ten minutes? The description in this talk of the Bible as a five-act play is an adaptation from a proposal made by N. T. Wright, which was adapted in Samuel Wells, *Improvisation: The Drama of Christian Ethics*. There are a number of differences between the Wright version and this version, notably that in the version presented here, abbreviated from the one in *Improvisation*, Jesus occupies the third act rather than the fourth, the fall is not accorded its own act, and the fifth act, heaven, or consummation, is separate from the act in which lies the church.

The alert participant will notice there's a degree of tension between the story as presented here and the story assumed in talk two. In talk two the incarnation – God being with us – is the purpose and original choice lying behind the whole story, and almost requires a prologue, rather as John's Gospel has a prologue before the established story of Jesus begins. But it's not a tension that needs to distract participants. After all, the story told in talk two still retains the features of all five acts.

Embracing all five acts dispels the tendency, inevitable in an introductory course, to focus so much on Jesus that the rest of the Bible besides the Gospels seems more hindrance than help – mere background for the enthusiast. By focusing on the moral significance of each of the five acts, it becomes clear that one can't make sense of Jesus without the context of creation, Israel, the church and heaven. The emphasis in this talk is less on the story the Bible tells – a story it would be daunting to summarize in such a short account – but on the key moves the story makes, and thus on the key things the reader discovers. This is a long way from the notion of the Bible as provider of short passages as food for daily devotional reflection; instead it's a claim that the Bible addresses the most profound questions about human existence in a way that proclaims the centrality of Jesus for meaning and truth.

The talk includes many questions. These are designed to make the Bible live as a document that addresses still-pressing issues, like how God will act if various things go wrong. The idea is not to see the Bible as a given story, locked in the past, in a time when human understanding of science was limited and commitment to verifiable facts was loose, but to see the Bible as a dynamic engagement with questions we still long to find answers to, and an inducement to follow the Bible's logic in discerning where to find those answers.

Describing the five acts enables the storyteller to identify what it means to get the wrong act. The description of moving from a one-act play to a five-act play is a succinct account of what it means to be transformed from a secular world view to a Christian world view. The contrast is blunt and designed to be memorable. The closing treatment of what it means to get the wrong act gives the participants a taste of what it means to think theologically. They can put the categories they've been given to work identifying common missteps in and widespread misconstruals of the Christian story.

It's unlikely that participants can rapidly process all this information so as to ask considered questions during the reflection time. More likely, the host may encourage them to surface matters about the Bible that linger and need further clarity. These may be factual ('Who wrote the Bible?' 'When was it compiled?') or more impressionistic ('Do people believe all those stories?' 'What about the bits where God seems so angry and vengeful?'). As in other places, these are not questions with simple answers. What matters for the host and storyteller is not that they fear such questions and therefore research plausible answers but that they welcome such questions as invitations to deeper engagement.

Six: Mission

If any of the sessions is the 'big reveal' that constitutes the distinctiveness of this course, it would be this one. But the participants may not realize this until they've attended session seven, and perhaps also eight and nine. It may seem strange to step aside from the transmission of the great themes of the faith and spend a whole session on a particular understanding of social interaction that's not universally subscribed to or even especially well known in Christian circles. So it may need some explanation.

COMMENTARY ON TALKS

For those who understand being with as central to the reason why God created the universe, why God came among us in Christ, and how we shall spend eternity with God, a session offering a greater understanding of the notion of being with, and how it contrasts with other models of interaction, is no detour. Instead it's an insight into the way the persons of the Trinity relate to one another, and how those dynamics play out in human relationships. The session is entitled 'Mission' because once the participants have a sense of the main components of the faith, they are bound to wonder how these elements affect the human condition – in particular those who suffer or are oppressed. Addressing social disadvantage and injustice is not an afterthought to the course, or a subject simply to be pursued once the main tenets of faith have been understood. Rather, the connection needs to be made from the outset that Christianity shapes how one addresses all such issues.

We are made to be with God, ourselves, one another and the creation, and this is how we anticipate experiencing eternity. In heaven there will be no more problems to fix: there will be no more for – only with. Thus our calling is to live God's future now by embodying today the life that we hope to inherit beyond our death. The attention given in the talk to the other three models is largely to highlight the significance of being with. It's not that there's no place for working for – there are some things it's a delight and a pleasure to do for one another, invariably when a relationship of trust already exists and there is some expectation of reciprocity wherein the favour will be returned. Likewise working with is in many cases very appropriate and in some respects constitutes an honoured dimension of being with. But being with is the definitive way God relates to us, and in heaven becomes the only way.

Thus an understanding of being with is crucial to grasping the nature and destiny of humankind and the glory and purpose of God. The two converge in the person of Christ, who is God fully with us and us fully with God. And it's fundamental to appreciating what this course is trying to do, which is to give participants such a profound experience of being with one another that they come, perhaps in retrospect, to recognize that this way of being together is part of what it means to be with God.

In such a short talk it's not possible to outline all eight dimensions of being with: presence, attention, mystery, delight, participation, partnership, enjoyment and glory. Even in a longer talk they would be a challenge to assimilate at one go. But the talk does identify three: mystery, delight and enjoyment. Enjoyment summarizes all eight, and could not be omitted. Mystery and delight are particularly apt for this course because mystery refers to the way God perceives us as a wonder to be explored rather than a problem to be fixed, and delight builds on our assets rather than highlighting our deficits. Both epitomize what the course method is trying to convey. In fact the eight dimensions of being with represent our best evaluative criteria for what 'success' looks like – in discipleship, ministry and mission, and in this course. At the end of the course, we want people to feel, 'Everywhere else in my life I'm used; here, in this course, I've discovered what it means to have been enjoyed.'

The notion of being with is articulated in many books, notably Samuel Wells, *A Nazareth Manifesto: Being with God*, and elaborated further in others, such as *Incarnational Mission: Being with the World* and *Incarnational Ministry: Being with the Church*; the account given here is an abbreviated version of that to be found in the Introductions to both the latter two books.

Seven: Cross

For those already familiar with Christianity, particularly for those shaped significantly by a more conservative outlook than is offered in this course, talk seven can be the most transformative moment of all ten sessions, and in some cases truly cathartic.

There are broadly five conventional notions of the atonement:

- The first focuses on Jesus' birth and suggests Jesus recapitulates every key moment of human life in order to 'raise' it. Jesus saves us by re-enacting every aspect of our human existence, setting right what was out of joint. Thus Adam disobeyed God by eating from the tree, whereas Christ obeyed God by dying on the tree.

COMMENTARY ON TALKS

- The second focuses on Jesus' life, proposing that in his kindness and generosity, in his ministry to outcasts, sinners and the sick, in his close relationship to the Father, in his prophetic confrontation with those who kept people under oppression, and most of all in his selfless and faithful journey to the cross, Jesus offers himself as the one who transforms our hearts to follow in his steps in the way of sacrificial love.
- The third concentrates on Jesus' suffering and argues that humanity had accumulated an unpayable level of guilt before God. Humanity therefore deserved eternal punishment. But through a unique act of grace, God sent Jesus to face this punishment in our place. This is sometimes known as penal substitution.
- The fourth considers Jesus' death as a sacrifice. The failure of humanity to do justice before God creates a terrible imbalance in the moral universe. Only humanity *must* pay the debt but only God *can* pay the debt. Hence the God-human, Jesus. When Jesus dies, he repays the debt of honour with interest, and it is this interest, known as merit, that humanity can access through the sacraments, and thus find salvation. This tends to be the predominant Roman Catholic view.
- The fifth thinks of the resurrection as like a victory in battle. Death cannot hold Jesus; he destroys death and opens out the prospect of eternal life by rising from the grave. The resurrection of Jesus brings about our resurrection by dismantling the hold of death not just once but for all time. Jesus' resurrection doesn't just save the individual soul but transforms whole societies by dismantling all the social, economic and cultural forces that oppress people.

None of these theories has been endorsed by the universal church, or appears in the creeds. What they all have in common is that they assume the word 'for'. Jesus lived, suffered, died and rose for us. The seventh talk in the Being With course extends the notion of 'with not for' to its understanding of the cross. This is partly out of a conviction that the manner of salvation should be consistent with its purpose: if Jesus came to bring reconciliation between God and humankind, now and for ever, metaphors of violent conflict, cruel punishment or agonizing sacrifice can't be the way God shows what love truly means. It's also partly influenced by the question of suffering and evil: if Jesus came to take away suffering and evil, and died for us to make it so, how do we account for the fact that suffering and evil are very much still with us? Their persistence moves us to consider that the meaning of the cross lies elsewhere.

But the most significant impulse to renarrate the cross in the language of with lies in the most poignant of all Jesus' seven last words: 'My God, my God, why have you forsaken me?' Scholars have often pointed out that these words quote the first verse of Psalm 22, which is in the end a hopeful psalm. This misses the point. These words offer a transformation of our understanding of the cross, from a job done on our behalf by Jesus to the revelation of Jesus' utter solidarity with us at any cost. It requires no grand theory of cosmic justice or any ancient notion of sacrifice. It simply requires us to contemplate the logical outworking of God's original choice never to be except to be with us.

How the participants digest this account of the cross may depend significantly on whether and to what extent they have prior familiarity with any or all of the conventional theories of the atonement noted above – particularly the third and fourth, which focus on Jesus' suffering and death. The aim of the talk is not to criticize the conventional theories but to present an approach in keeping with the character of God displayed in Jesus' coming among us and promise to be with us always, and with the nature of the Trinity as three persons so perfectly with one another that we call them one; and in keeping with the nature of the course as participants have experienced it.

This talk is an abbreviated version of the introduction to Samuel Wells, *A Cross in the Heart of God: Reflections on the Death of Jesus*. Further reflections on the cross in the same spirit can also be found in *Hanging by a Thread: The Questions of the Cross*.

COMMENTARY ON TALKS

Eight: Prayer

The eighth talk displays the rhetorical approach of the talks in the course perhaps better than any of the others. It attempts to offer a good deal of insight about how people truly think about their own lives, such that most participants should be able to identify with at least some elements of the descriptions expressed here. But it gives a shape to those descriptions in the form of a conversation that, while taking significant effort, should be well within the scope of any of the participants – and if not, then at least within the scope of what they could imagine being involved in. Eventually it turns out that our true conversation partner is God, and our conversation partners, while wholly valid in themselves, are also training us in how to converse with God. Which is why the session is entitled 'Prayer'. The power of the talk lies in feeling satisfied three-quarters of the way through that it's already covered enough ground to provoke and inspire – and then to find the real point is yet to come.

The exercise described is one offered and practised with numerous groups and audiences over more than a decade. If yours is a group that takes readily to doing homework between sessions, it would make a very suitable project to ask each member to carry out. But what you don't want to do is create a situation where one member feels so embarrassed at not having completed the assignment as not to attend the next meeting. So it can be an invitation, but it can't be a requirement.

The talk profoundly affirms the shape of the course. The subtle message is that at the end of one of the course sessions, the participants should feel as though they have prayed. The host may choose whether to point this out or leave it for the participants to surmise. The talk seeks to show the ultimate unity of theology and ethics, spirituality and practice. Learning to be with God and learning to be with one another are ultimately the same kind of learning.

Perhaps more than the other talks, this is one in which the storyteller might want to study the crucial words carefully, so as to have mastered their significance before giving the talk. 'We think of our neighbour … and we think about their wealth – and we think of the wonder of God's universe. And we call that praise. We think of our neighbour in their poverty ... and we call that intercession. We think of ourselves in our poverty and of everything we could have done differently, and we call that confession. We think of ourselves in our riches, and all the blessings of our life, and we call that thanksgiving.' The whole talk hangs on these words, but as it's easy to get the concepts mixed up it's important to take them slowly, so the participants can hear the extent of what the words are saying.

This talk is an abbreviated version of a sermon that's included as the Epilogue in Samuel Wells, *A Nazareth Manifesto: Being with God*.

Nine: Suffering

Whereas the previous talk looked like a talk about being with but turned out to be about prayer, talk nine looks like a talk about prayer but turns out to be about suffering. It deliberately chooses a form of suffering that has no prospect of ending in any way other than death, that is, not an illness from which one can hope to recover, an injury that will in time heal or a disability one finds a way to live with. The debate about how, in a world created, overseen and entered by a good and all-powerful God, there is still suffering, is as old as faith itself. For Christians, the answers aren't to be found so much in the nature of creation or the assumption of some kind of a fall, rather they lie with Jesus. The real questions are:

- If Jesus came to take away suffering and evil, how come they still seem to be very much with us?
- If God will bring the story of the universe to an end and usher in a heavenly realm of being utterly with us, when sorrow and crying and pain will be no more, why does God not do that now?

The answer this course implicitly offers is, yet again, that God is committed to being with us rather than to a project of working for us, and so God in Christ enters into our suffering alongside us rather than simply taking it away. But the great weight of Christian reflection and practice has fallen less on the question of why there is suffering than on the issue

COMMENTARY ON TALKS

of what to do about it. In some ways the whole history of the church can be seen as a response to the challenge of what to do about suffering. So this talk takes the same trajectory, and considers what we most want God to do about suffering, and thus how we intercede.

The significance of this talk is that it's the only place in the course where the conversation hints at something beyond being with. The resurrection prayer is evidently a working-for prayer, and the participants should be sufficiently familiar with the terminology by now to recognize that for themselves. The incarnation prayer is a being-with prayer, and again, that should be clear to the group. But the transfiguration is something more than just a being-with prayer. It adopts the method of overaccepting, which is described earlier in this book as a key dimension of what the course is seeking to be and to do. What would often be regarded as setbacks or disappointments are fitted into a much larger story, in which they are transformed into occasions of grace – epiphany moments in which God's glory is revealed.

People have often spoken of this talk as the most helpful of the ten. That may well be because it addresses a question they were already asking before the course began: 'How do I pray in the face of tragedy and sadness?' It's also sometimes the case that participants have formerly had experience in a church that prays the resurrection unreservedly and without exception, and has little recourse to alternative understandings should the outcome not be the one for which they have earnestly prayed. In fact, this can be one of the biggest reasons people turn away from faith, feeling let down either by God or by those who have portrayed God in somewhat one-dimensional working-for terms. Whereas the other talks are creating an appetite for something they trust the participants will find truly satisfying, this talk is usually the most readily received because it's meeting a need they already knew they had.

It's important not to present the material in a way that seems to dismiss the resurrection prayer. That's not the intention of what the storyteller is saying. The point is that the resurrection prayer is not the only way to intercede lovingly, and in some circumstances may be asking for something that is not just unusual but defies all medical experience. Then the point is to display the richness of first the incarnation prayer and finally the transfiguration prayer. If participants truly grasp what the transfiguration prayer is reaching for, they may come close to perceiving the glory that is the eighth dimension of being with (see page 14).

This talk is an adapted version of the closing section of Samuel Wells, *A Nazareth Manifesto: Being with God*.

Ten: Resurrection

The tenth talk is seeking to do several things. Like the first talk, it's about resurrection, so it bookends the whole course with the central claim of Christianity, that the incarnate Christ, fully human, fully divine, is so utterly with us that he dies, as we do, but remains so utterly with God that death cannot hold him – and so through these two facts promises us we shall be with God for ever.

But by the device of going through six alternative great days, the talk offers a succinct summary of the whole Bible, including elements of all five acts of the five-act play outlined in the fifth talk. All six days could lay plausible claim to being the day that contains all the others:

- the creation, because without it there would be no other days;
- the exodus, because it proclaims and demonstrates that God is about setting us free from all that oppresses us;
- the covenant, because it embodies God's will to be in relationship with us, and shows that commitment is as important for God as it is for us;
- the incarnation, because it is the day God is with us like never before;
- Good Friday, because here we discover there are no lengths to which God will not go and no hardships God will not endure to be with us;
- the Last Day, because everything that made no sense in history is finally woven back into the story and redeemed.

The claim made in this talk is that Easter Day contains all six of those days. This claim becomes a way of explaining the theological significance of Jesus' resurrection and the way it crystallizes and fulfils every element of the Bible, before and after. Note that it explicitly avoids language

COMMENTARY ON TALKS

of victory and conquest. Instead, its principal metaphor is that of yeast whose urge to expand makes it impossible for any stone across the tomb to resist. A violent defeat of death would in the end suggest there was violence in God. This account has no violence but a portrayal of God's grace as something that's deeper, longer and higher than any human limitation or perversity.

It's intended to be an inspiring end to the course, a crescendo that brings the series of ten talks to a rousing conclusion. But it doesn't need to be delivered in a loud voice. It's more of a life-giving whisper than a sergeant major's wake-up call. It's based on a gentle understanding of God's ways that mimics the tender knowledge the storyteller has gained about the participants from what they've shared in the ten weeks of the course.

In a subtle way the talk is encouraging participants to get to know the Bible better, not 'to be a better Christian' but because by knowing the Bible better they will better comprehend the full wonder of who Christ is. They will come to realize that the many perspectives and insights the Bible gives on Christ are almost inexhaustible. It's moving participants away from a consumer mentality of 'What can this God do for me?' to a devotional entering of the mystery of a universe saturated with the love of God. Just as this talk is encouraging participants to see every part of the Bible casting light on the wonder of the resurrection, so that spirit extends to understanding every moment of human, and in particular their own, experience as shedding wisdom about how God is seeking to be with us. Thus in the end the wonderings and the talks are pointing to the same reality: God's constant longing and invitation for us to join the dance of being with.

This talk began as an Easter Sunday sermon and is published as the Epilogue to Samuel Wells, *The Heart of it All: The Bible's Big Picture.*

3

Commentary on Wonderings

One: Meaning

The wonderings for the first session engage with what it means to be released from the prison of the past and the fear of the future.

- *I wonder if you've known what it feels like to be set free.*
- *I wonder if you've known what it feels like to be in prison.*
- *I wonder what it's like to know there's something in the past that you don't need to worry about any more.*
- *I wonder what it would be like to know the future isn't going to hurt you.*

People often ask why the course doesn't start in a more low-key, relaxed, unthreatening way – to which there are several answers. One is that the host is aiming to take the participants more seriously than they take themselves, and at the same time show genuine and profound interest in who they are and what experiences have shaped their lives and faith. Starting with something significant is a way of saying, 'If you really want to get to the bottom of what this Christianity thing is about, you've come to the right place.' But like almost all the wonderings, it doesn't need to trigger great heart-searching. For the first wondering, for example, it's perfectly appropriate to respond, 'I remember leaving my primary school and being so glad I'd never have to go back', or, 'When I passed my driving test, I felt I could go anywhere.'

One thing the host will realize is that participants aren't always ready to share something that's clearly in their mind. It's fine to be silent as participants evaluate whether to share something and how to say it. But it's also fine to move on: in several cases the next wondering isn't enormously different, and a member of the group might say, 'I'm actually going to say something that applies to the previous wondering as well.' In this session the second wondering is closely related to the first, in order to give people two opportunities to cover the same ground, or a chance to offer two different stories from their life.

More than most subsequent wonderings, these four are very specifically related to the two main parts of the talk – about the past (faith) and the future (hope). This is partly to get participants' hearts and minds engaged with the subject, and thus more prepared to hear what the storyteller has to say; but also to furnish examples and stories that can easily be integrated into the talk.

Two: Essence

- *I wonder where you find most meaning in life.*
- *I wonder if there's an idea that encapsulates what you think life is all about.*
- *Tell about a time you wanted something to last for ever.*
- *I wonder what's the best thing in life.*

The second talk asks participants to think deeply about eternity. Sometimes people say 'That's a bit deep' – but there's no reason to apologize for that. What we're trying to model is how to accompany participants in their most profound explorations and anxieties – the origins of life, what happens when we die, the meaning underlying all things. To think about such things alone can be fearful. To be together and not delve into such things, or to do so in a graveyard-humour style of 'Who knows?' is a missed opportunity. What could be better than to name and ponder the most mysterious things in life with others in an atmosphere of trust, discovering that there can be a framework that makes sense, it doesn't have to disrupt everything you hold dear, and it's OK for there to be something no one knows the answers to?

The first wondering illustrates the importance of sending the wonderings to participants a few days ahead of the session. Many people, faced cold with a wondering such as this, would be reluctant to commit themselves to a succinct response. But note the wondering says 'where you find' not 'what you think': it's not as threatening, because it's not asking for a definitive epigram. It's inviting a narrative – assuming that each participant does indeed find some meaning in life, and returns to that place to continue to discover more meaning. Note also it's in the present tense, so the assumption is that participants are not simply recalling an event that showed them something important, but are narrating something they are in the habit of finding and expect to continue to find in the future. (That's why it's a wondering and not a 'tell about'.)

The second wondering also aims to get to the heart of participants' convictions without doing so in a threatening way. It does this by inviting participants to quote or cite another person's wisdom, rather than disclose their own. Again it illustrates the importance of giving participants some preparation time.

The third wondering moves to personal anecdote. If it had been the first wondering it would have been more threatening, but having exchanged locations and ideas the participants have warmed up enough to take the risk of sharing something personal. But as with most wonderings, it's not asking for a superlative: it doesn't have to be the very best moment of your life – it can simply be a job that was going really well, or a holiday that came at the right time during an otherwise difficult season.

Then the fourth wondering should elicit ready responses. Unusually for a wondering, it actually is a superlative. But again it doesn't require a profound answer. 'Walking the dog at the end of a busy week' is perfectly acceptable. So is 'Sitting round the dinner table with all my grandchildren'. By the end of the wonderings the conversation will have generated several thoughts for the storyteller to work with, but also have got the group into the right balance of intensity and relaxed trust to be ready for the talk.

COMMENTARY ON WONDERINGS

Three: Jesus

- *I wonder who you'd say 'your people' are.*
- *I wonder who you feel Jesus' people are.*
- *Tell about a time you found solidarity with an unexpected group of people.*
- *I wonder if there's any way in which you feel Jesus was like you.*

The third session has a more practical feel. The first wondering gives participants a chance to share with the group something of their story and context, particularly in ways that might not immediately be apparent. This may include the community in which they grew up, which might be very different in location and culture from where they are now; or a community of identity, if they identify as from a minority of any kind; or a community of interest, if they have a passion or pursuit that isn't shared by everybody. There's an adversarial element lurking beneath the wondering – a hint that these are people who understand you in a way the rest of the world doesn't, or who see the real you in a way the rest of the world can't.

Having started with personal experience, and some sense of being in tension with the majority of one's culture, the second wondering may take things in a direction participants weren't expecting. It's easy to assume Jesus was one who floated straightforwardly across class and race, with no abrasive tension in relation to any social group, as one who encountered no prejudice and faced no discrimination. But this wondering invites participants to see Jesus as a real human being, perhaps with a strong accent, arguably in a minority, not always an easy social fit. It also makes a transition to the present day and provokes the imagination to guess from which social group Jesus would choose his disciples as he went for fishermen, tax collectors and retired terrorists in and around Galilee.

The third wondering can go in either a very personal or a more casual direction. If a participant has a unique story to tell about identity, trauma or transformation, this offers an opportunity to share it. But again, it doesn't have to be a time of revelatory disclosure. It can be a lighter story of an unusual moment in life where one found something in common with a group from which one was previously, and subsequently, more distant.

The fourth wondering brings all the three previous ones together. It's always good to remember that when a person is silent it's less often because they dislike the wondering or are baffled by it, more often because they are exploring how their own reaction forms an appropriate answer, and whether they feel comfortable sharing that answer in this setting. So by offering a fourth wondering that touches on territory covered by the second wondering, the host might well elicit what had been an unformed contribution to the earlier conversation that now sits more comfortably in the shape of the wondering time as a whole. By the end of this wondering period participants should have explored ways Jesus is both similar to and different from them.

Four: Church

- *Tell about a community that you've been part of and the ways it brought out the best in you and others.*
- *Tell about the ways it relished difference and diversity and addressed failure or undermining actions.*
- *I wonder what kinds of qualities a community needs to be sustainable.*
- *I wonder what kinds of qualities you believe you bring to a community.*

The fourth session explores church by inviting participants to share their experience of community. It starts with the positives, noting one's own investment and the ways communities flourish by bringing forth creativity and energy from their members. It also gives participants a chance to share about a significant period in their lives to which they might return in later sessions. The wondering about diversity highlights how a healthy community distinguishes itself from a dysfunctional one by the way it turns points of tension into opportunities for renewal rather than reasons for destruction. The second wondering can be pivotal: if people have had previous experience of the church, and have left, a likely

COMMENTARY ON WONDERINGS

reason is the way that community handled difference or failure. One of the things the person might be particularly alert to is whether this emerging community, the group itself, can negotiate such things differently. If there's a sad story to tell, this is where it's likely to surface.

The third wondering shifts the emphasis from narrative about communities in the past to reflections on what makes a good community. If the atmosphere has become negative in the sharing of painful histories, this lifts the mood and gives participants the chance to change into constructive mode. If it were the first wondering, it might provoke a baffled silence, but on the back of genuine sharing of the good and the troubling, the group has built enough raw material to make some worthwhile generalizations. While in general commenting on one another's responses is not encouraged, this may be an occasion for the host to extrapolate from one or more of the participants' contributions, and say, 'I wonder if what Rosie said about the person that finally told the truth is something that every community needs.' This is inviting participants to find wisdom in each other's testimony.

Then the wondering period concludes, again constructively, by inviting participants to see themselves not as consumers of community but as its contributors and perhaps leaders. The last wondering is about beginning the transition from the group to the church more broadly. Having seen what communities need, how they flourish and what makes them go wrong, participants are now challenged to name the gifts they themselves bring to the table. It's a chance to balance affirmation and challenge. The effect of the whole wondering period is to leave the group members the wiser for what their own experience has taught them and ready for what the storyteller has to say.

Five: Bible

- Tell about a story you've loved a long time.
- Tell about a story concerning your family that everyone has heard too many times.
- I wonder if you've ever felt there was a story that had no place for you.
- I wonder if you've ever felt there was a story that did have a place for you.

The fifth session is in some ways the most challenging, because it covers territory where the participants have most diversity in the information they already have, and where there's the greatest danger in applauding those who have some knowledge of the Bible and making those who don't feel small. For this reason, the wonderings don't talk about the Bible at all.

Instead, the emphasis is on story. The Bible is not just story – it includes much else. But the emphasis of this session is to enable participants to grasp the notion of the Bible as one great story, about past, present and future, and to recognize that being a Christian is to take up a part in that story – specifically, within Act Four.

So the wonderings approach story from different angles. The first is a typical wondering, in that it can be answered with a profound or a trivial response, it can disclose something vital about a participant or can just as easily be kept at arm's length. It can be a story from the Bible or from anywhere else. It can be *War and Peace* or *Thomas the Tank Engine*. The response may require the host to do a little prompting: for example, if the respondent simply names a story, the host may invite the participant to say a little more about the story and why it's so special.

The second wondering offers the possibility of humour, but doesn't require it. It may be what the uncle always says at Christmas dinner, or it could be one person's sense of their own victimhood that crowds out the whole family's ability to embrace any other kind of pain. It's the first time in the course that explicit mention has been made of family, and this may trigger some sharing of complex dynamics within participants' families of origin.

The third wondering moves from comfortable and familiar territory to experiences of exclusion and marginalization. They aren't necessarily painful – everyone else wanting to watch the World Cup final when you have no interest in it may not be something that you experience as genuine exclusion; but being a woman in a church tradition where women aren't allowed to be ordained may for example be a profoundly alienating thing, and being a Black person who finds no reference to people like oneself in histories of the country one lives in may be telling you something very uncomfortable about belonging.

The last wondering takes all the discomfort of the previous wondering and turns it round into the joy of true belonging. This isn't simply designed to be a bland account of feeling at home, but a more far-reaching narrative of having at one stage being excluded but now belonging – as with the Gentiles in the New Testament. If the first couple of responses have taken the former approach, it may be helpful for the storyteller to model a more helpful contribution – for example: 'When I moved schools for the sixth form, for the first time I met people who liked reading books and discussing ideas, and I realized I wasn't so strange after all.'

Six: Mission

- *Tell about an occasion when someone has been so keen to fix you that they've missed a moment when you just wanted to be heard and understood.*
- *Tell about when you worked on a project with a group of people and got satisfaction from achieving it.*
- *I wonder if you've ever wanted to tell someone to stop moaning about a problem and go and do something about it.*
- *Tell about a time when someone truly heard, understood and cared about you in the midst of a crisis.*

Being with as a concept begins with the negative experience of some not being with you: the first wondering invites members of the group to articulate such an experience. It's worth offering plenty of time to this wondering, not to create a litany of resentment but because the more participants are in touch with what it's like to feel isolated despite there

BEING WITH: COURSES AND COMMENTARY

being someone who was well placed to connect with you, the more this crucial session of the course will make sense. It may require the storyteller to model such a response, perhaps by telling a story from childhood when a need for connection was missed and the demand to fix and cure took over.

The second wondering is about working with, or what in the language of the dimensions of being with is known as partnership. In typical wondering fashion, this can be profound and self-disclosive or straightforward and undramatic. It could be performing a play or finishing a professional contract; it may equally well be completing a round of family therapy in the light of one member's eating disorder, or assisting a group of women who'd met through a women's refuge in telling their stories through an art course.

The third wondering subtly turns the first one around and enables the participants to articulate the kind of pressures and impulses that can make it so difficult to be with another person. Some people simply are challenging to be with: they have unpleasant habits, they are self-absorbed and saturated with self-pity, they are locked in self-doubt or self-hatred. The point about this wondering is to move participants towards recognizing how remarkable it is that God genuinely wants to be with us – since we are all of those things, to some degree. Expressing frustration and failure, as well as exasperation and impatience, is an important part of coming to understand what being with actually entails.

Finally there's an opportunity to share a genuinely positive experience of being on the receiving end of being with, as the opposite of the first wondering. Unlike most wonderings, this invites a serious, honest response, and is hard to dismiss with a non-disclosive or light-hearted contribution. For that reason, there may be a degree of silence before the first response emerges. Again, it's vital not to be frightened of silence and to trust that participants are simply evaluating what they feel comfortable saying – in particular, to what extent they are able to share the nature of the crisis in which a person was with them, or who that person was.

By the end of this wondering, participants should already have described many of the features of being with, and the storyteller should have a good deal of material to integrate into the talk that follows.

COMMENTARY ON WONDERINGS

Seven: Cross

- *Tell about a time you had to give up something good to keep hold of something else that was also good.*
- *I wonder what it's like to feel you're without everything.*
- *I wonder what it's like when a close community breaks apart.*
- *Tell about when there was something you thought you could rely on – and then you couldn't.*

The first wondering, like many others, can evoke light or very honest responses. It's not unknown for a participant to talk about walking away from a relationship, or choosing one profile over another on a dating app. It changes the default that exists for many people, that there's a right or good thing to do and if you just do that, all will be well. Instead, it embraces a more complex world where there may be more than one – perhaps several – possible directions to pursue, and sometimes you don't know before, during or even after whether you made the best decision, or how to evaluate 'best', or whether you can even imagine how things would have turned out had you acted differently.

The second wondering is perhaps the most challenging in the whole course. It would be simpler to say, 'I wonder what it's like to die', but this wondering is subtler, and also recognizes that one dying person may have some things another does not – a happy life to look back on, the company of loving friends or relatives, for example. It may take some time for participants to respond to this wondering, but it's worth the wait. If they can get into this intellectual and emotional place, the talk that follows will mean so much more.

The third wondering may trigger disclosures that are among the most profound moments of the whole course. It invites stories of real pain, where hopes have been raised, trust established, dreams envisioned – but then everything unravels. This can be within a family, if something deeply troubling takes place and can't be navigated, or within a work setting or church or neighbourhood. It connects with the disintegration of the community of disciples after the Last Supper, when all flee and leave Jesus to his fate. It's always vital for participants to hear each other's stories without rushing in with superficial reaction, matching accounts or proposed solutions, but never more so than in this case: the host may wish simply to say, 'Thank you, Jack, that story sounds like it goes very deep for you.'

The fourth wondering may elicit more accounts similar to those told in response to the previous prompt, but it's more open-ended. It can, for example, relate to oneself – one's health, most obviously – or to a collective experience like that of the Covid-19 pandemic. It's designed to place the group in a condition of corporate sensitivity to vulnerability, but in an atmosphere of trust where that's not so much painful as tender. This is the best condition in which to hear what the storyteller has to say. It's unlikely on this occasion that the storyteller will include much material from the wonderings in the talk: the talk should speak for itself.

Eight: Prayer

- *Tell about a way you are rich.*
- *Tell about a way you are poor.*
- *I wonder what most amazes you.*
- *I wonder what it's like to feel part of a whole bigger reality.*

What makes these wonderings satisfying is that the first two so closely mirror the conversation described in the talk. Of course the participants don't know that yet, so the satisfaction only arises at that later moment. But recognizing one's own wondering as it shows up in the talk can be an affirming experience that leads to closer listening and engagement. The first wondering has layers to it and, unlike a number of other wonderings, participants may be moved to give more than one response as they discern deeper and deeper layers to their experience. As is the case in the talk that follows, the idea is to break through stereotypes about privilege and comfort and arrive at more profound matters of identity and relationship, creativity and purpose. There's also a challenge in starting with rich rather than poor: most people are more aware of their deprivations than their blessings, regardless of their economic security or state of health. Rather than be a source of embarrassment, the presence in the group of people from significantly differing social backgrounds can stimulate participants' imaginations to name issues that transcend class and race.

The third wondering is intended to engage participants' sense of wonder, which is the most fertile soil for prayer. It's a very broad invitation, but by being phrased as a superlative it's given a degree of focus. The superlative shouldn't be taken as an indication that participants may offer only one response. It's an example of where the various responses are likely to trigger further responses as the group develops a kind of corporate wondering.

The last wondering is again very broad, seeking as it does to stimulate reflection both of the breadth of the universe and of the company of heaven – the communion of saints, the Trinity, the angels and archangels and all that the believer hopes to lie in store. It's been said that prayer is the experience of joining the worship of God by the angels that is going on all the time. Such an insight captures the kind of breadth this wondering invites.

Nine: Suffering

- *Tell about a difficult time that proved to be a learning or growing time.*
- *Tell about something helpful someone said to you in a challenging situation.*
- *I wonder what you would say to someone whose closest relative had just been diagnosed with Alzheimer's.*
- *I wonder if you've ever prayed for something and not got it.*

It's conventional to portray suffering as a problem to be solved – either practically through humanitarian or medical intervention, or intellectually through theories about free will or the fall. This session treats suffering as a mystery to be entered. The first three wonderings gradually deepen the context, pushing a little further each time. The first isn't necessarily about suffering at all. Getting your first job as a teacher may involve a steep learning curve, but developing the arts of lesson-planning and classroom management can hardly be described as suffering; it's nonetheless a hard time that many would later look back on as a growing time. This introduces participants to the idea that an experience can be both negative and positive at the same time.

The second wondering makes the first conversation more dynamic, by recalling a spoken intervention by a third party that reframed a challenging experience. Note it's something somebody else said to you – not something you said to someone else. This isn't the moment for proclaiming one's own sagacious insight, or for anyone in the group to do so. This turns a difficult time into an opportunity for growth and relationship – a problem shared becomes a mystery entered.

Then the third wondering turns attention from the past to the future, from what someone says to you to what you say to someone else. Meanwhile the context becomes much more specific. This is now a very real situation, in which you don't get the choice to have nothing to say – your friend has shared some news and you're obliged to respond in some way. This offers a good sense-check on whether participants have truly comprehended and digested the sixth session; it would be a little alarming if, having been part of the group for this long, they were eager to rush in to find a solution.

The fourth wondering places the conversation in the context of intercessory prayer. This may evoke deep doubts and bitterness about the experience of so-called unanswered prayer; just as likely, it may invite disclosure about a context in a participant's life or wider circle that gave rise to such a prayer. If so, this is the best possible environment for such a disclosure to take place: surrounded by trust and understanding, but in a context where it should be clear that the group's role is not to rush in and fix it. Again, this should create exactly the right atmosphere in which the talk can best be heard.

COMMENTARY ON WONDERINGS

Ten: Resurrection

- *Tell about a truly wonderful day.*
- *Tell about a day when something that had seemed a burden was turned into a gift.*
- *I wonder, if you could change one thing about the world, what it would be.*
- *I wonder if you have one possession that somehow contains or represents a lot of other possessions.*

This final session allows for and invites expressions of joy that have arguably been few in previous sessions. While the consistent theme of the course is that God is with us through the hardest things of all – suffering and death – this last session affirms that, in the end, Christianity is about joy. To get in touch with what joy might feel like, we begin with narrating a truly wonderful day. For some this will be an episode from childhood, perhaps romanticized; for others, a moment of transition or celebration, like a wedding day; for others again, it may come from a realization that scarcity has turned into abundance, and the recollection might be about events that seem mundane, yet are seen with fresh eyes.

The second wondering changes the focus from unambiguous joy to the recognition of how a difficult story can be reconfigured – either by events or by reflection – into an occasion for learning, growth and gratitude. This is a different kind of celebration because it includes pain and lacks the simplicity of the first kind, but also because it's perhaps more honest, and therefore richer to describe. Here participants are sharing how they went through a profound change of perspective: a kind of conversion. Conversion is more than a change of perspective, but invariably includes one, or many. This might be a moment when a participant realizes their whole view of life and everything has changed during the course.

The third wondering can provoke some fascinating responses: one participant waved aside conventional answers about suffering or death, and simply said, 'I'd abolish the word and the mindset that produces the word "normal".' While asking participants to express such views at the start of the course is likely to prove unsuccessful, since they don't yet know how valued are their experiences and identity, and how much trust the group can establish, doing so at the end of the course is invariably rewarding, since it can produce an unexpected response that doesn't always sit predictably with the person the group has got to know. It's designed to ready the group to hear about the one change that changes everything else.

The last wondering more explicitly connects to the tenth talk by getting participants into the imaginative place where one thing can represent many other things. It may not be an easy wondering to respond to, but it does a lot of work simply in being expressed because the capacity of the resurrection to encompass the whole Bible and indeed everything about Christianity is what the talk is about.

4

Being With Global

Commentary

This version is designed for younger participants, or participants for whom English is an additional language. The original course is the most complete version. This edition misses some nuance and detail for the sake of brevity and ease, while retaining the overall meaning.

Being With starts with the assumption that people are full of experiences of the Holy Spirit from the day their lives begin. Giving space to hear these experiences as participants identify and articulate them is the heart of a Being With course. It's a privilege to be with each person as they realize that they are full of experiences of God, and that these experiences are valid regardless of how lucid the participant is in response to the wonderings or to what extent the participant is able to digest every element of the story. Entry to a Being With course does not depend on educational attainment or prior knowledge. We all have stories to share, no matter what our experience. Having those experiences cherished in the way a Being With course does, while cherishing the experiences of others in the same way, is for many a transformational process.

As with all Being With courses, the point of the talk is not necessarily for participants to understand all the detail of the argument, but for them to participate and remain open to what the Spirit might be saying. It is a spiritual experience rather than a lesson. The point of the Global version is to continue to give this space to others for whom terminology or detail in the original version might prove a distraction.

Here are some notes specifically for younger groups:

BEING WITH: COURSES AND COMMENTARY

- We suggest 13+ age. Some of the concepts and language would be difficult for most under-13s to understand, and might therefore inhibit their full participation.
- Leaders should be aware of the safeguarding policy under which they are working.
- In light of the safeguarding policy, it's important for leaders to consider who they are inviting, and the dynamics of the group. Sticking to age groups – 13/14-year-olds or 15/16-year-olds in the same group – may work better in encouraging peers to share and speak, and in managing safeguarding.
- The wonderings invite people to speak vulnerably. As with every Being With course, it's important to be mindful of this and vigilant about possible pitfalls, paying close attention and following up with individuals as necessary.
- Some people may find silence awkward. Silence usually arises not because participants have nothing to share but because they're not sure if they trust this group to honour what they want to share. In groups of young people, being very clear about the role of silence from the outset is important. It's usually enough simply to explain that there might be silence, the leaders are fine with the silence, and it is to be expected.
- In response to the wonderings, it's sometimes helpful for the host to be prepared with personal examples that can be helpful to aid explanation of words or phrases in the wonderings that might be misunderstood.
- The weaving of material by the storyteller from responses to the wonderings, drawing in participants' experiences so that they can illustrate the talk, can powerfully animate the story.
- We suggest that these groups are led by experienced hosts and storytellers, who have the ability to manage group situations and maintain silence so as to hold space for individuals to share.
- These conversations may bring up issues for individuals; this can be amplified if they are younger. But this should not discourage leaders. On the contrary, these are precisely the kinds of conversations leaders should be seeking to have with young people they are responsible for being with.

One: Meaning

- *I wonder if you've known what it feels like to be set free.*
- *I wonder if you've known what it feels like to be trapped.*
- *I wonder what it's like to know there's something in the past that you don't need to worry about any more.*
- *I wonder what it would be like to know the future isn't going to hurt you.*

We live in the present tense. But, in many ways, we don't. A lot of the time we are concerned by things in the past we can't change and things in the future we can't control. These are the things we worry about in bed at night. These are the things that trouble us as we try to focus on the here and now.

We're stuck between two challenges: our powerlessness to change the past and our fear about how the future will turn out: the prison of the past and the fear of the future. They can leave us asking, 'How can I live in the present in the here and now? How may I be free?'

What does the Christian faith say? Two central convictions. One about the past and one about the future.

The first conviction is about being released from the prison of the past. It's forgiveness. Forgiveness doesn't change the things that have gone wrong. Forgiveness doesn't change our histories. But it does mean our histories don't have any power over us. Forgiveness transforms our past from an enemy out to hurt us to a friend available to help us. Instead of resenting or feeling powerless, we can find wisdom and peace. That's the work of forgiveness. It transforms the prison of the past.

Imagine being released from the prison of the past. It's almost beyond our imagination. It's half of Christianity.

Here's the second conviction. It's about the future – the life everlasting. Everlasting life doesn't tell us what the future will hold, but it promises us the future won't hurt us. Everlasting life doesn't guarantee certainty, but it offers confidence and trust. Everlasting life doesn't cancel the reality of death and suffering, but it gives us life beyond death, comfort beyond suffering, connection beyond loss.

Without everlasting life, we're stuck with the fears that keep us awake at night. We can't help ourselves trying to make everything all right amid changes and threats. We can't stop seeking some kind of meaning despite the cruelty and waste that seems to ruin everything. We scroll our phones or turn the music up loud to block out our despair of the future.

Everlasting life means we don't need to have the last word; evil is real, but it won't have the ultimate say; death is coming, but it doesn't cancel the power of God; we are fragile, but whatever in us is of God will be transformed into glory.

The name for the point at which forgiveness and everlasting life meet is resurrection. Resurrection restores the past and opens out the future. It's the fulfilment of the old story and the beginning of a new one. Because of resurrection, death is no longer a wall; it's now a gate. Death turns from nothingness and loneliness into true awareness and never-ending togetherness. We call it heaven. We're given back our future as a gift. Everything is possible.

Imagine for a moment the gift of everlasting life. Feel it slowly undo all your worst fears. Let it set you free. Let it give you indescribable joy. It's the other half of Christianity.

The heart of it all is forgiveness and the life everlasting. If you have those, nothing can finally hurt you.

Every part of our lives – past, future and present – now has a new name. The past – what we trust God has done – we call faith. The future – what we believe God will do – we call hope. The present – what God embodies and makes possible – we call love.

Two: Essence

- *I wonder where you find most meaning in life.*
- *I wonder if there's an idea that sums up what you think life is all about.*
- *Tell about a time you wanted something to last for ever.*
- *I wonder what's the best thing in life.*

We can think of two kinds of reality. One kind lasts for ever; the other kind lasts for a limited time.

Let's start with what lasts for ever. When we identify the heart and soul of something, we use the word 'essence'. When we speak of what's permanent, for ever, what has always been and will always be, we call it essence.

Then there's what doesn't last for ever, whether it's around for a week, a year, a hundred years or a million years. It decays, it dies, it disappears; it's limited. But it still matters. So we call it 'existence'.

We human beings aren't part of essence. We don't last for ever. We fade, decay and die. We're part of existence. We're not 'essential': there could be a universe without us. We may think we're eternal and permanent, but we're not; we exist for a while and then we're gone.

There might have been no existence. There might only have been essence. So, why is there existence? Because essence – which we often call God – chose for there to be existence. God chose for there to be something different, something changing. That's us: the universe, creation, everything that exists.

God could have chosen not to create existence – really, that would have seemed more likely. Yet here we are. Existence is a gift: we did nothing to bring it about – either existence in general or our own. We creatures, who are limited, and so often shift and change, and who live only a short time, and in such fragile bodies, get to enjoy everything; yet we haven't done a thing to make it possible.

But this raises the biggest question of all: why is there something rather than nothing? Why is there not just essence? Here we find the wonderful claim of Christianity. On one starry night, moved by migration, in a hostile political area, surrounded by animals, from a young mother living homeless in a strange town, essence came into existence. God came to be with us – not just as God, but also as that fragile, additional, changeable bit of creation called humanity. The Word became flesh.

Here we discover why there is existence. Because God always intended to be with us. That's what the word 'Jesus' represents: God's purpose from before existence to be with us. That decision and desire set in motion the whole mystery of the universe. Jesus isn't an afterthought that came into existence when everything was going badly wrong; Jesus is the whole meaning and purpose of existence in the first place. Jesus is the reason we exist: so God could be with us – really with us, with us as existence as well as essence.

But we haven't yet reached the best bit. As we said, not only has God come to be with humankind but God becomes human too. Jesus is fully human and fully God, and through him we realize what God's final purpose always was: to invite us into everlasting life, into essence – into what lasts for ever. Jesus is God stretching out a hand and saying, 'Abide with me' for ever. God's hand stretches out, in Jesus, and invites us to become part of essence – to abide with God for ever, even when all existence has passed away. From essence into existence back into essence. What an amazing gift.

And so here we are – tiny, pointless, passing specks in a universe that's bigger than we can even imagine. But the personal quality of essence has chosen to become one of us, because of a desire to be with us, in a tender, humble, understanding relationship. And this is the reason for existence in the first place.

And this being with, which we call Jesus, shows us a new way, a new example for being in relationships, relationships that are inspired and fuelled by the Holy Spirit. The ultimate purpose is for God not just to share existence with us but to draw us finally into essence and dwell with us for ever. So every time we form, establish, restore and deepen understanding, relationships with one another, we demonstrate the way God seeks to be with us and glimpse the glory of God.

Three: Jesus

- *I wonder who you'd say 'your people' are.*
- *I wonder who you feel Jesus' people are.*
- *Tell about a time you felt connected to an unexpected group of people.*
- *I wonder if there's any way in which you feel Jesus was like you.*

We know about Jesus because the details about his life are recorded in four short books we call Gospels. Each of the Gospels tells pretty much the same story: Jesus comes into the world, is raised in a town called Nazareth, says and does amazing things that inspire many and threaten some. Those words and actions lead to his arrest. He's nailed to a cross and dies in great pain. But two days later he's raised from the tomb, appears to many and eventually returns to heaven.

The gospel stories describe three kinds of relationships Jesus has: first with his close friends who followed him and wanted to be like him; second with the crowds who heard his extraordinary words and witnessed his dramatic actions; and third with the authorities – the people who disagreed with him and eventually put him to death. Let's look more carefully at these relationships and what they show us about Jesus.

Jesus calls around him 12 followers, known as disciples. He instructs them in his way of being with one another and being with God. These disciples fumble and fail, fear death, lack imagination and even betray. But Jesus points to a new way, a new hope of restored community, demonstrated by his death and resurrection.

Then there's the crowd. These displaced and excluded people see Jesus' miracles, hear his stories, learn from his example and follow his path. When he enters Jerusalem on a donkey, they wave branches and sing 'Hosanna'. But just five days later, they shout for him to die and choose to save the terrorist Barabbas instead.

The third relationship is Jesus' conflict with the political and religious leaders who often misused their power. Eventually we see that the real power lies with Rome. It's the Romans who finally kill Jesus – only for him to dismantle even Rome's control over life and death.

BEING WITH: COURSES AND COMMENTARY

This story is our story. Our story divides into the same three strands as Jesus' story – companionship, poverty and conflict: all dimensions of his being at the heart of God.

First, we're part of a group of companions. A Christian is called into relationship with a community. We may already have close family ties. Following Jesus may strengthen existing relationships, or it may test and challenge them. But either way, we're called to make new, close and accountable relationships with members of the church.

Then, second, we're in relationship with those who are oppressed – those that in some way experience poverty. There are many ways to do this. A relationship that brings about real change is friendship, because to be a friend is to say, 'I am allowing myself to be changed by knowing you.'

Third, we see Jesus' confrontation with the authorities of his day. Jesus is constantly having debates with those who hold power. There's plenty wrong with the world, and we have a choice how to respond: go and put it right yourself or, if you can't, make life uncomfortable for those who can until they do.

And just as for Jesus' story, these three strands – of accountable community, friendship with those experiencing oppression, and challenge to the powerful – all unite in the fundamental story, which is what God asks of us, our sharing in the mystery of God, and our entering the glory of God. Jesus' relationship with God was expressed, discovered and revealed through accountable community, friendship with those who are poor and challenge to the powerful. Why should ours be any different?

Our temptation is trying to have the big story, walking with God, without the stories that make up that story – joining in with accountable community, friendship with the those experiencing oppression, and challenge to the powerful. Our temptation is wanting to have all the benefits of Christian faith without any of the costs. Our temptation is trying to have God without Jesus.

But what happens if we focus on only one element of these three? If we only focus on our companions, we will miss transformation through becoming a friend of those experiencing disadvantage. If we look only at the oppressed, we may neglect challenging those in power. If we put all our effort into challenging authority, we may forget that our own integrity lies in being in accountable community and walking alongside those experiencing oppression.

All of these are temptations to have just part of the gospel – just the community bit, just the poverty bit or just the shouty bit – without the rest. You could say they're temptations to make a Jesus out of our own needs and desires. They take one of the three strands and ignore the big story. It's the temptation to have Jesus without God.

The gospel leaves us with these three questions:

1   Am I a disciple? Am I a member of a group of people who hold me to account and challenge me to put my life where my mouth is?
2   Am I a friend of those experiencing disadvantage? Have I said to someone, 'I am allowing myself to be changed by knowing you'?
3   Am I confronting oppression? Am I asking difficult questions of those who dominate, manipulate, exploit and neglect?

These three questions put feet on the gospel.

Four: Church

- *Tell about a community that you've been part of and the ways it brought out the best in you and others.*
- *Tell about the ways a community enjoyed difference and diversity and addressed failure.*
- *I wonder what kinds of qualities a healthy community needs.*
- *I wonder what kinds of qualities you believe you bring to a community.*

One of the early enemies of the church became its leading supporter. His name was Paul. He taught that the church is like a body, and each member is like an eye or an ear or a hand. The foot can't say to the hand, 'I don't need you', nor can the eye say to the rest, 'I'm the whole body.' Paul underlines that the weaker members of the body are vital to the health and welfare of the body. What does he mean?

Richard Adams' 1972 novel *Watership Down* tells the story of a dozen rabbits that search for a warren to call home. Each of the communities the rabbits encounter has its own political system. The warren at the beginning of the novel is like a traditional society. The rabbits run away from that warren because they think it's about to be destroyed by humans. A second warren the rabbits find is an oppressive society. One general keeps all the other rabbits in a state of fear. A third community of rabbits resembles a modern rich and selfish society. Food is plentiful and the living is easy. But the rabbits have lost the ability to find their own food and, more seriously, to tell the truth. They can't bring themselves to realize that they're under the spell of a farmer who feeds them but also snares and kills them one by one. The fourth warren is the one the rabbits found for themselves on Watership Down.

The rabbits discover many things through their adventures. The most important thing they discover is that they need each other. One of the rabbits is big and strong; another is quick-thinking and imaginative; a third is speedy; a fourth is fiercely loyal; a fifth is a good storyteller. The key rabbit is the smallest and clumsiest, who yet has a sixth sense that anticipates danger – like the destruction of the original warren. What makes this group of rabbits so significant is that they find ways of using the gifts of every member of the party so that they're never short of wisdom and intelligence about what to do next or courage and strength to do what's needed. The group of rabbits lives and moves and thinks as one body rather than as a dozen separate bodies. There can't be an idea that is good for one of the rabbits but not good for all of them.

This group of rabbits teaches us about what it might mean to be church. First, the rabbits in the story are longing to get to the point where they can say, 'Phew – that's it. We've made it.' Well, there is no such point. The moment never comes. When the dozen refugees meet the easy-living rabbits who live the good life, they can see quite quickly that those drunk rabbits have lost what it takes to be a community, to tell the truth, and ultimately to survive. The church becomes one body as it is bound together on its common journey. It's always a work in progress.

Second, the mixture of the church is a strength, not a weakness. The group of rabbits only survived because it had rabbits with different gifts, different strengths, different visions for what they were doing and where they were going.

Once, there was a monastery where the monks were constantly at each other's throats, fighting and being cruel to one another. One night a mysterious visitor knocked at the monastery door and made a brief but clear announcement: 'One of you is Jesus Christ.' The atmosphere in the monastery changed overnight. Suddenly each monk treated every other monk with awe and wonder, not sure which one was Jesus but knowing Jesus was among them. They'd learned what it means to be church – to treat one another as we would treat Jesus.

The third thing we learn from the rabbits of Watership Down is that being one body isn't about ignoring differences, letting acceptance emerge and making all the rabbits dull and grey. What saves the rabbits at crucial moments is their willingness and commitment to listen to one another, to hear each other out when they have stories, worries, doubts or hopes. Being one body is probably more painful than going our separate ways. We can waste time avoiding each other and not listening to each other's experiences and stories. But there isn't anything more important for us to rush off to. A Christian telling another Christian 'I have no need of you' is really telling Jesus, 'I have no need of you.'

Five: Bible

- *Tell about a story you've loved a long time.*
- *Tell about a story concerning your family that everyone has heard too many times.*
- *I wonder if you've ever felt there was a story that had no place for you.*
- *I wonder if you've ever felt there was a story that did have a place for you.*

The Bible tells a story in five parts. The first is creation. The second is about Israel, the ancient tribe chosen by God. The third part is Jesus, God-with-us, the centre of the story. The fourth part is the church, which is where we're living today. The fifth part is the end, or heaven. Let's look more closely at each part, and then two things that can go wrong with this story.

In creation, God is the creator. God says, 'There's too much love to keep to myself.' God says to us – to each one of us – 'I made you this way because I wanted one like you.' Our main purpose is to glorify and enjoy God for ever. And yet we creatures use our freedom badly. We see how God turns freedom into a relationship of love, and how humanity turns this relationship into a prison.

The second part is Israel. This part of the story is what Christians call the Old Testament. God says to a drifter named Abraham, 'Follow where I show you.' Abraham says yes. The rest of the Old Testament is a love story in which Abraham's descendants go between the desire to hide themselves from God and the joy of being close to God. God will not leave them alone – which is both a promise and a warning. The questions are: 'How can God win this beloved nation back?' and, 'Can the people walk in God's ways?'

The third part is Jesus. This is the central part, the middle of the drama. In this part of the story we find answers to some of the questions from the previous part. God's character is fully revealed; God enters the drama. Jesus is both fully human and fully God. He is the expression and fulfilment of the covenant made earlier in the story. But this isn't the end; Jesus' chapter shows the tension of human intimacy as well as the collision course of death and evil with the love of God. Jesus is killed on the cross, but is then raised from the dead.

Christians are in the fourth part, the church. We see the church receiving all it needs to be Christ's body in the world. It is given gifts of the Holy Spirit, scripture and actions like Eucharist and baptism to keep it going and to grow. This chapter leaves us with questions. Will these gifts be enough? How will God communicate beyond the church and how will that communication help?

Still to come is the fifth part. Only God knows when this last part will happen. We believe we'll see all secrets revealed. In God there are many surprises – but no shocks. The God who'll be fully revealed in part five will not be different in character from the God who was revealed in part three. The face on the cross is the face on the throne.

There are two kinds of mistakes we can make about this five-part story. The first is to think there's only one part. If there's only this one part, everything must happen now. The past has nothing to teach us, and there's no future to transform us. The five-part drama calls Christians to faithfulness instead of success or being effective. Faithfulness ends up being success because we are not at the end of the story: we are in part four, with part five still to come, Christians can (and do) fail, because they can trust that the Holy Spirit will put right their mistakes. Their faithful failures point to their faith in the story and its author.

The second mistake is to put ourselves in the wrong part of the story. If we think we're in the first part, suddenly we're in the role of creator. There's no experience to learn from, no story to join, no drama to enter. This is the desire for independence, to be a self-made individual. If we're the creator, no one else's rules apply to us: everything must be discovered, named, assessed for ourselves.

What if part four is very long, and the church still has thousands or millions of years ahead of it? Perhaps we *are* the early church, still arguing over the details, and rightly so. Somehow we can't lose the insistence that we are at a decisive stage near the end of the story. The five-part story proclaims that humanity has already, in part three, done the most terrible thing possible by crucifying Christ. Humans are neither the creators nor the completers of God's story.

Six: Mission

- *Tell about an occasion when someone has been so keen to fix you that they've missed a moment when you just wanted to be heard and understood.*
- *Tell of a time you worked on a project with a group of people and got satisfaction from achieving it.*
- *I wonder if you've ever wanted to tell someone to stop moaning about a problem and go and do something about it.*
- *Tell about a time when someone truly heard, understood and cared about you during a crisis.*

Imagine the little word 'with' is the most important word in the Christian faith. Let's explore four ways to make the world a better place.

BEING WITH: COURSES AND COMMENTARY

1   Working for is where I do things and they make your life better. Working for is the normal model for improving the world. It says the way to address disadvantage is for those with skills, knowledge, energy and resources to put those things to use to improve the situation of those who are struggling. It says those with the advantage have abundance, have more to give, and through education and training should use what they have to work for as many people as possible. The 'needy' then are defined by their deficit – by what they don't have; if they have skills, knowledge, energy or resources, these are not noticed or used. Working for sees problems and focuses on fixing those problems; then it moves on to the next problem, of which the world is never short. One challenge is that people seldom like being seen as a problem to fix or solve.

2   Working with is a different model. Like working for, it gains its energy from problem-solving, identifying targets, overcoming obstacles and building momentum as more is achieved. Working with gathers around a common cause: initially drawing together the like-minded and those of similar social standing, but eventually making partnerships across social divides, like religion and class. By forming networks and creating a movement where it's possible for everyone to win, working with gets things going and helps those disadvantaged to feel they belong.

3   Being for is more concerned with getting the ideas right, using the right language, having the right attitudes. Being seen to do or say the right thing is the vital thing. Much of this is good, but in its desperation that Something Must Be Done, it can become clear that it's for somebody else to do the doing. Remaining silent on important issues is viewed as disengagement or withdrawal. Being for can often mean people who don't fully understand the complexity of situations nonetheless feel the need to say or do something.

4   Being with rejects the idea of problem and solution. Its main concern is the situation that has no solution, the scenario that can't be fixed. It sees the most significant moments of life like this: love can't be achieved; death can't be fixed; pregnancy and birth aren't a problem needing a solution. When it comes to social disadvantage, it

believes one can't really solve people's problems – doing so damages and hurts relationships with others. Instead, one must accompany people while they find their own methods, answers, approaches – and celebrate and enjoy their true identity, which is not wrapped up in what one judges to be their problem. Being with starts with people's assets – what they have; not their deficits – what they don't have. It seeks never to do for them what they can perfectly well, perhaps with encouragement and support, do for themselves. But most importantly, being with seeks to model the goal of all relationships: it seeks to delight in people, enjoying them for their own sake, right here, right now, not trying to get them to do something or be something they are not.

To summarize:

- Working for is where we do something for someone else. Our dentist works for us and does what we can't do for ourselves.
- Working with is where we do something with someone else. A climate coalition brings members of different organizations to campaign around a common issue.
- Being for is where we do something for another at a distance. We post on the internet our solidarity with victims in a distant war.
- Being with is where we focus not on using a relationship to achieve some other goal, but on enjoying relationship for its own sake, as the purpose of our created existence and a glimpse of heaven.

See how these categories map on to Jesus' life. Jesus works for us by forgiving sins and opening the gates of everlasting life – achievements concentrated in his suffering, death and resurrection, and anticipated in earlier healings and miracles. Jesus also spends perhaps three years, largely in the north-eastern province of Galilee, calling, forming and empowering followers, formulating a message for them to share, building alliances and confronting hostility. One can see the 'saving' as working for, focused on a week in Jerusalem; and the 'organizing' as working with, spread over those years of public ministry. But that still leaves perhaps

30 years in Nazareth, give or take a spell as a baby in Egypt. And here's the question: if Jesus was all about working for, how come he spent around 90 per cent being with (in Nazareth), 9 per cent working with (in Galilee) and only 1 per cent working for (in Jerusalem)? Are those percentages significant – and do they provide a template for how Christians should engage with the problems of society? Surely Jesus knew what he was doing in the way he spent his time; or do we know better?

Seven: Cross

- *Tell about a time you had to give up something good to keep hold of something else that was also good.*
- *I wonder what it's like to feel you're without everything.*
- *I wonder what it's like when a close community breaks apart.*
- *Tell about when there was something you thought you could rely on – and then you couldn't.*

If there's one word that sums up Jesus' story, that word is 'with'. Jesus' ministry, above all else, is about being *with* us, in pain and wonder, in sorrow and in joy, in quiet and in conflict, in death and in life. Jesus is God incarnate, which means he is fully God and fully human.

God, Christians understand, is three inseparable persons: Father, Son and Holy Spirit, with Jesus as the second person. The Father, the Son and the Holy Spirit, called the Holy Trinity, are so *with* one another that it seems they are *in* one another. We still call God one, even though God is three, because God is the perfect balance of three, each part is *in* the other part perfectly – so perfectly they are *with* each other, not overpowering one another, just utterly *with* one another.

Good Friday is the day we see the very heart of God and the very worst in ourselves. On Good Friday, Jesus is executed by being hung on a cross. Jesus' words at this moment are, 'My God, my God, why have you forsaken me?' At first, this looks like the last in a list of horrible events. Jesus' companions leave him, his friend Peter denies he knows him, Judas betrays him, now God the Father rejects him. It's a list of desertion.

BEING WITH GLOBAL

The events leading up to Jesus' crucifixion dismantle with. Jesus is left without all those he worked so hard to be with – his companions, those experiencing oppression, the authorities. All of them have deserted or betrayed him. Jesus is still with us, but we, at this most precious moment of all, are not with him.

But these abandonments are nothing compared to the one that really matters. The cross is a unique event. It's not unique because of how much pain Jesus felt or how much love he'd previously expended. It's unique because the Holy Trinity is the truest example of with, and at the moment of Jesus' death, that with is, for a brief moment and for the only instant in all time, lost. This is the most heart-breaking and terrifying moment in all history.

Jesus has given everything in him for the cause of being with us. He's given so much – even despite our determination to be without him. And yet he's given beyond our imagination, because for the sake of our being with the Father he has, for this moment, lost his own being with the Father. And the Father has longed so much to be with us that he has, for this moment, lost his being with the Son, which is the essence of his being.

Here we are, at the central moment in history. Jesus, the incarnate Son of God, has to choose between being with the Father and being with us. And he chooses us. At the same time the Father has to choose between letting the Son be with us or keeping the Son to himself. And he chooses to let the Son be with us. Can you believe it? That is the choice on which our life everlasting depends. That's the centre of the Christian faith and our very definition of love: to choose us, whatever happens.

These two wonderful discoveries, the Father's losing the Son for us and the Son's losing the Father for us, rattle our bones because they make us wonder, 'Is all then lost?' – not just for us, but even for God. If we don't experience a shiver of this greatest of all horrors at this point then we haven't allowed ourselves to really take it in. But this deepest of fears is what will find an answer two days later, when we find that neither sin nor suffering nor death has the last word. With is restored at Easter and, on the day of Ascension, with has the last word.

Is our separation from God really so profound that it pushes God to such lengths to reverse and heal it? We don't want to believe it. But here it is, in front of our eyes. That's what the cross is – our cowardice and cruelty confronted by God's wondrous love. Is being with us for ever really worth God going to such lengths to secure? Now, that's the most awesome question of all. It takes us to the heart of God's identity, and the heart of our own. Can we really believe God thought we were worth it? Are our worthless lives worth the Trinity setting aside the essence of its identity in order that we might be with God and included into God's life for ever?

Jesus' cry is one of agony that to reach us he had, for a moment, to let go of his Father. What is our cry? Our cry is one of grief that we were not with him. It's a cry of astonishment that he was, despite everything, still with us. And it's a cry of conviction and commitment that we will be with him from now on and for evermore.

Eight: Prayer

- *Tell about a way you are rich.*
- *Tell about a way you are poor.*
- *I wonder what most amazes you.*
- *I wonder what it's like to feel part of a whole bigger reality.*

Here are four parts of a conversation you might have with someone.

Tell me about the ways you are rich. Tell me about the ways you are poor. Let me tell you about the ways I am poor. Let me tell you about the ways I am rich.

Maybe the conversation might go something like this. You say, 'Tell me about the ways you are rich.' And your friend says, 'I appreciate the way you see me for what I am and not just for what I'm not. My childhood was difficult, I didn't do well at school, but I feel rich in the way I learned to read people and understand them. I feel rich in the wonder of the birds and their song and the dawn and its beauty and the pouring rain and its refreshment. I've never had much money, but I have a wealth of friends and somehow there's always been someone who's stepped in to help me when I couldn't manage everything myself.'

And then you say, 'Tell me about the ways you are poor.' And your friend might say, 'You're probably expecting me to talk about how I can't pay the rent and can't find a job. But when I feel really poor is when I see a person who's a lot worse off than me and I feel I can't help them. I feel poor when I see a newcomer to this country trying to make their way and I can't speak enough of their language to be useful to them. The real times I feel poor are when I think of my daughter who died when she was two and I was 19 and I miss her with more sadness than I have in my whole heart.'

And then you say, 'May I tell you about the ways I am poor?' And your friend might say, 'I'd never thought of someone like you as poor.' And you say, 'I felt I had to apologize for being a girl. All my life I've struggled with comparing myself to others. I've always hated my brother, even though I've never told him and anyone would think we were the best of friends. I wonder if I've ever trusted anyone enough to show them who I really am.

'But I'm also rich. I've always had the ability to concentrate. I can listen or read, or even be silent and pray, for hours. And I can paint. I can paint a watercolour, I can paint a miniature, I can paint a wall, I can paint a face, I can paint anything and make it laugh and dance and spring to life. I share my heart through my paintbrush.'

When the two of you have shared your riches and your poverty with one another in this way, you may want to leave it there. But you may choose to go a little further.

Your friend may say to you, 'Let me tell you about how you're rich. You're rich because you don't have to spend every waking moment of your day earning money, so you've got time to do beautiful things and walk with people who are in trouble. You're poor because you've never found a way to love your brother. You're poor because you don't have enough people like me around you to tell you the truth about yourself.'

And then you may find the courage to say to your friend, 'You're rich because your laugh is infectious and exciting. You're rich because every child you ever meet loves you. You're rich because you've already been through the worst that life can bring so you live without fear. But you're also poor. You're poor because you really want to do something useful for others but you can't find a way to do it.'

If you have the first kind of interaction, that's called a conversation. But if you have the second kind of interaction, where you talk about each other, that's more than a conversation. That's called a real relationship.

Poverty is a mask we put on a person to cover up their real wealth. And wealth is a disguise we put on a person to hide their poverty. Those we call the rich are those in whom we choose to see the wealth but are more reluctant to see the poverty. Those we call the poor are those in whom we choose to see the hunger but are slower to see the profound riches. God takes that in each of us that is rich and sees through it to our poverty. And God takes our poverty and sees past it to our deeper riches.

And every day we enact these words before God. We think of our neighbour, in person, society and globe, and we think about their wealth – and we think of the wonder of God's universe. And we call that praise. We think of our neighbour in their poverty, and all that's wrong in the world, and we call that intercession. We think of ourselves in our poverty, and everything we could have done differently, and we call that confession. We think of ourselves in our riches, and all the blessings of our life, and we call that thanksgiving. These are the four parts of prayer. Praise, intercession, confession, thanksgiving. The riches of the world, the poverty of the world, the poverty of ourselves, the riches of ourselves. These are the ways we make that courageous intimate conversation a daily act of renewal.

Have that conversation with someone this week. Make it the time you remember that Christ left his wealth and took on your poverty that he might make you wealthy in the way he is wealthy. Make it the time you discover another's poverty and another's wealth, and think about your own wealth and your own poverty.

But have that conversation with God every day. For that's what prayer is. Prayer is when we see God's wealth and God's poverty, and bring to God our poverty and wealth, and our neighbour's too. That's a daily conversation, in which our friendships, our lives and our world are being transformed.

Nine: Suffering

- *Tell about a difficult time that proved to be a learning or growing time.*
- *Tell about something helpful someone said to you in a challenging situation.*
- *I wonder what you would say to someone whose closest relative had just been diagnosed with an incurable disease.*
- *I wonder if you've ever prayed for something and not got it.*

Let's imagine a conversation. You say, 'Hi. We haven't talked for a while. How are you, what's up?' And you catch up on this or that. And then, just as you're finishing, she holds your forearm, her tone changes and is more serious, and she says, 'Say a prayer for my dad, will you, he's sick, in fact he's really sick. It's been a while, but it is getting serious now.' And you look into your friend's eyes, and in them you see the cost of what is required to keep going, and of what it has taken just to put that pain into words, and you say, 'I'm sorry. I'm so sorry. This must be such a bewildering time for you. Of course I'll pray for your dad. And I'll pray for you too.'

But then you've made a promise, a promise you must keep. How exactly do you pray for a person in such a situation? What words can you find to wrap around this tragedy, in which lives and souls unravel and there's no sign of the dawn?

There are two conventional ways to pray for your friend and her dad. I'm going to call the first way resurrection. It's a call for a miracle. You say,

'God, by the power with which you raised Jesus from the dead, restore this man in mind and body, make him himself again, and bring my friend the joy of companionship and the hope of a long and fruitful family life together.'

There's a big part of you that wants to pray this prayer. You love your friend. You see how watching her dad disintegrate before her eyes is breaking her heart. You want God to show some compassion, some change, some action. In the back of your head, you maybe have a sense of some Christians who seem to pray for resurrection all the time, and you wonder if you should have more faith and expect God to do amazing things every day. But you've also seen hopes dashed, and a part of you can't even say the word 'heal' because it seems to be asking for something that just isn't going to happen. That's the prayer of resurrection. You know Christianity's founded on it, and you know it's what your friend most longs for – but sometimes you just find it too hard to say.

But that's not the only kind of prayer. The other conventional kind of prayer is the prayer of incarnation. It's a call for the Holy Spirit to be with your friend and her father. It's a recognition that Jesus was broken and alone, on the brink of death, and that this is all part of being a human being, all part of the deal from birth. Our bodies and minds are fragile, frail and sometimes feeble. There's no guarantee life will be easy, comfortable or fun. The prayer of incarnation says,

> 'God, in Jesus you shared our pain, our foolishness and our bad luck; you took on our flesh with all its weakness. Visit my friend and her father now: give them patience to endure what lies ahead, hope to get through every trying day, and companions to show them your love.'

The resurrection prayer expects God to do all the work, this prayer stirs us into action ourselves. If we say, 'Send them companions to show them your love', is anyone better placed to be a companion than us? Your friend is aware that the prospects for her father are awful. What she's really asking is, 'Help me trust that I'm not alone in all of this.' Chances are, you can help her with that. But you'd hardly be human if you didn't feel powerless and inadequate considering what she's going through.

Resurrection and incarnation aren't the only kinds of prayer. They say pretty much all we want or need or ought to say. But there's a third kind of prayer – a prayer of transfiguration:

> 'God, in your son's transfiguration we see a whole reality within and beneath and beyond what we thought we understood; in their times of bewilderment and confusion, show my friend and her father your glory, that they may find a deeper truth to their lives than they ever knew, make better friends than they ever had, discover reasons for

living beyond what they'd ever imagined, and be held in your grace like never before.'

This is a different kind of a prayer. The prayer of resurrection has a boldness about it – in the face of what seem to be all the facts, it calls on God to produce the goods and turn the situation round. It has courage and hope but there's always that fear that it has a bit of fantasy as well. The prayer of incarnation is honest and steady about the present and the future, but you could say it lacks a little hope.

Maybe this is your real prayer for your friend and her father. Maybe this is your real prayer for yourself, amid whatever it is you're wrestling with today. Not so much, 'Fix this and take it off my desk!' Nor even, 'Be with me and share in my struggle, now and always.' But something more like,

'Make this trial, this difficulty, this problem and pain, a glimpse of your glory, a window into your world, when I can see your face, sense the mystery in all things and walk with angels and saints. Bring me closer to you in this crisis than I ever have been in calmer times. Make this a moment of truth, and when I cower in fear and feel alone, touch me, raise me and make me alive like never before.'

Ten: Resurrection

- *Tell about a truly wonderful day.*
- *Tell about a day when something that had seemed a burden was turned into a gift.*
- *I wonder if you could change one thing about the world what it would be.*
- *I wonder if you have one possession that somehow contains or represents a lot of other possessions.*

Imagine you're in heaven and you're looking back on eternity to select the very best day of them all. We could suggest six finalists. Let's take them in chronological order.

First, the day of creation. It's got fabulous fireworks. It's the day the imagination of God was expressed and turned into existence. Do you think the whole history of the universe was contained in embryo on this day, like a tiny egg that contains a person's whole future?

Our second candidate is the day of the exodus. This is the great day when God parted the Red Sea and took the descendants of Abraham, who'd been enslaved in Egypt, to freedom. Just imagine the joy and discovery that nothing was impossible with God. Great day.

Our third candidate is the day of the covenant, when God gave Moses the Ten Commandments and God's commitment to Moses' people was made real in promises and guarantees and tangible forms of loyalty and love. It was the day that defined what it meant to be God's people and how to live for ever in peace with God and one another. It was the original mountain-top experience.

Then, fourth, Christmas. The day we discover God loved us so much as to become one like us. God coming at Christmas was the reason for creation. God made the world in order to be with us in Christ.

But then in at number five there's Good Friday. On the day of the exodus God's people saw God's power. On Good Friday we see God's love. Hands that threw stars into space to cruel nails surrendered. What wondrous love. Could any day be better than this?

Well, here's a candidate. What about the Last Day? The last day of all. The day when Christ comes back. The day when everything wrong in all the history of time gets set right, when all who have been broken are seated on thrones, and all who have lost their lives in tragedy find deep joy. The day when everything that creation was meant to be but never quite became is transformed and creation is changed from glory into glory and showered in wonder, love and praise. Beat that.

Maybe we can beat that. Early in the morning, depending on which version of the story you read, there was one woman, or three, or two men, who went to a tomb. It's a day that began as one of the saddest-ever days. But before breakfast time it had turned into the Day of Days – not just the greatest day of them all, but the day that contained all the other six. Just see how this day, this holiest, most astonishing and wondrous day, is all the other six days wrapped into one.

It's another creation day because, look, it's Jesus and Mary, a man and a woman in a garden, just like creation, and it's a day of limitless possibility. It's the exodus again, but not just for a small number of people long ago; this time it's for everyone, for ever – people released from being enslaved. And it's another covenant. The first covenant showed Israel how to stay close to God: this one shows everyone that nothing can separate us from the love of God – not even death itself. Whatever we throw at God, however deeply we reject God, however much we seek to bury or destroy God, God will find a way back to us. That's the truest covenant of all.

And look how it's like Christmas all over again, but bigger. Everything the incarnation proclaims and embodies, the resurrection affirms twice over: God will be with us in Christ, not just out of original purpose but even when we have done absolutely everything to try and get rid of Christ. There is a new resurrected body. The human body has an eternal destiny. Easter is Good Friday again. Jesus is the good shepherd who has laid down his life for his sheep. And now this blessed morning he begins to go around gathering his flock, starting with Mary Magdalene. Good Friday shows us that God will be with us even if it splits God's heart in two. Easter shows us that nothing whatsoever can stop God being with us, not just at the most intense moment in history – but for ever.

And then finally Easter is the Last Day in miniature. Like the Last Day, Easter restores creation. Like the Last Day, Easter supports the oppressed, in this case Jesus, and exalts the humble and gentle. Like the Last Day, Easter is the enactment of every single one of the Beatitudes. Jesus is the pure in heart. Jesus is the peacemaker. Jesus is the one who hungers and thirsts for righteousness. Jesus is the one who is hated by all people. And on the day of resurrection, he's happy, he's blessed, he's called God's child, he's laughing.

This day, this wondrous, glorious, blessed, fabulous day – this day is the greatest day in the history of the universe and the story of heaven. This is the perfect seventh day, the day that comprises and epitomizes and embodies and expresses all the other six great days of all time. This is the day on which all the suffering, all the imagination, all the love, all the freedom, all the grief, all the justice, all the hope, all the wonder are combined in a mixing bowl, left behind a huge stone, and like yeast acting on a mixture, burst out, push that stone away because there's so much life there nothing can keep it in, no one can keep it down, no force in heaven or earth can stop it now.

This is the day. This is the great day. This is the glorious day. This is creation, liberation, incarnation and consummation all wrapped into one. This is the day when we stand on the shoulders of God, and say, 'I can see for ever!' This is Easter Day.

The Impact of Being With

In December 2022, retired social services administrator Marian Walker entered a church for the first time in five decades and, soon after, signed up to a Being With course that changed her life.

I was brought up as a Roman Catholic in a very devout family. Then my brother died when I was 21 and my mother died shortly afterwards. I drifted away from the church and didn't have any contact with it for the subsequent 50 years.

I've always felt there was a God but my Catholic faith had taught me that Christ died on the cross because I had sinned; I couldn't understand that, so I felt I could never be a Christian. I didn't feel I needed a church or a community. My plan, when I retired, was to live as isolated a life as possible. But I began to feel a need to receive communion again, so I turned up at my local church on Christmas Day 2022. Then I went back for Epiphany and heard this wonderful sermon and thought, 'That was written just for me.'

It just so happened that the Being With course was starting the following week. I signed up. I loved the format of it, and the safety of knowing that whatever I said was going to be accepted without comment. Every week I got something wonderful and truthful from the talks; I'd learn something that I'd been trying for 50-odd years to find out.

The week we came to the cross, I learnt the theory that Jesus dying on the cross as a sacrifice for our sins is just one theory among others.

BEING WITH

The teaching I heard on the course, that Jesus came to earth to be with us, and in fact that's why we were created, just felt true to me. I went to bed in tears thinking, 'Why did nobody tell me this before?' because, if they had, I wouldn't have spent five decades looking for a way to have a relationship with God when, really, there it all was.

I have learnt how to be part of a Christian community – to be with a group of people and listen, and be alongside them. There have been changes in absolutely every aspect of my life. I've got a future I didn't imagine I would have.

Being With answers questions that I think everybody spends most of their life looking for. To someone considering doing it, I'd say there's absolutely nothing to lose and absolutely everything to gain: more than you can possibly imagine.

Zac Koons is Rector of St Mark's Episcopal Church in Austin, Texas. He has run more than ten Being With courses since 2020.
I've taught a lot of classes and there's nothing else like Being With. Instead of trying to teach people about God, it tries to give them an experience of Christianity by experiencing God. It starts from the view that if God is real then everything that you've brought into this meeting, your whole history, is relevant experience with which to think through these questions.

Every single time I do a Being With session, I think, 'This is the best and most worthwhile thing I've done all week.' It's never boring. Each course follows the same roadmap and covers the same topics, but it's completely different every time – because the majority of the content in each session is determined by the people in the room.

The people who take part experience something really special. It changes their faith permanently and gives them a different vocabulary with which to look for God in the world, and in their lives and church. It's not about arriving somewhere else – it's about stopping and recognizing God right here.

It's fun to watch the people in the congregation who have taken Being With; they become like yeast in the dough – this wonderfully agitating presence that has a knock-on effect on the rest of the church.

THE IMPACT OF BEING WITH

The course is also extremely effective in meeting those people that grew up in church and at some point dismissed it, but now as adults are starting to think, 'Maybe I need to spend some time thinking about these questions.'

Every time we offer Being With, we put out a call in the neighbourhood asking, 'Are you looking for a safe space to explore big questions about meaning and suffering and God?' And it takes a kind of brave weirdo to accept that invitation.

Rebecca Bridges is an Episcopal priest who has served churches in both the US and Canada. Originally from Florida, she was ordained in 2019, having previously been a professor of Communication and Media Studies at Stetson University. In addition to hosting Being With courses, Rebecca has trained many people seeking to offer the course in their own parishes.

I led my first Being With course while I was associate rector of St Stephen's Episcopal Church in Birmingham, Alabama. We began just a few months after a traumatic incident for the church. In 2022, an attendee at a potluck dinner for older members of the congregation shot and killed three parishioners. Countless others were impacted because they knew those who had died, or because it had changed their sense of our church being a safe space.

Not all of what was shared during the course was about that incident, but it gave those who took part in Being With that fall a sacred space to share, particularly in the weeks when we shared about the cross, suffering and resurrection. Church could feel safe again.

Beyond that, I've had people tell me after completing the ten-week arc that Being With changed the way they listen to others; it had given them a new way of receiving what people share with them. More than one person reflected that they wished this is what church could always be like.

I moved to Toronto in 2023. That fall, I began co-hosting Being With trainings. I personally had experienced Being With as a gift; now I wanted to share this gift with others. I really believe both as a Christian and as a priest – and as someone with a lot of teaching experience – that the course opens up listening, meaningful conversations and deepening of faith. It's personally fulfilling to know that I'm placing this gift into more people's hands. I'm delighted picturing others around the world who will be able to experience this in their own communities.

I often tell people that, although it is described as a course, it's really more of an experience. What I'd say to someone considering running it is that you will be beautifully surprised by how generously people listen and share.

Being With has impacted the overall theological outlook that I bring into my preaching and my day-to-day relationships personally and in the parish. The whole idea is deceptively simple: Jesus came to be with us because God enjoys us and wants to delight in us. We can follow Jesus simply by being with other people. The course gives us practice in learning how to simply *be with*. The incarnational theology underlying Being With informs my whole approach to ministry.

After many years seeking acceptance from the church as a gay Christian, Wendy Young became involved in church leadership, recently co-leading a Being With course that has taken her a step closer to ministry.
I was brought up in the Dutch Reformed Church in South Africa, which was really strict and fundamentalist. I had a very strong faith from a young age, but I knew I was gay from about 12 and it was made very clear at church that I would go straight to hell if I didn't change that. I tried to find other churches, but there was nowhere I could be part of a church community and be myself. I didn't question who God was, but I did question where I fitted into his plan. It was really hard.

I came to the UK ten years ago because I fell in love with a Brit and came to live with her. I've always wanted to be in ministry, but being gay had meant that it wasn't possible. Then, a year ago, Tim our vicar said, 'You want to be in ministry, let's do it!' When he asked me to lead a Being With course with him, I was completely blown away. I never thought I'd have the opportunity to do something like that.

The very best thing about Being With is how it gets down to the very core of things straight away, like poetry. The people who took part were present with all of themselves from week one. It was a privilege, and so moving, to witness them start thinking about Christianity, their faith and their relationships with other people and with God.

THE IMPACT OF BEING WITH

All six people stuck with it. They are still friends and they are not alone in the world any more. Two of them came in very vulnerable and untrusting of others, and they've made really good relationships and come to church quite often. A third person who took part has asked to be confirmed. The thinking, feeling and wondering is an ongoing thing.

Being With is a bit of a miracle – it's perfect for the time and space that we're in right now. It fits with being more fluid in your thinking, in your relationships and your sexuality. I think it's going to be a sacred, mysterious tool that God uses.

For me, it opened up the fact that God is even bigger and more wonderful, and way more out of my comfort zone, than I ever thought. My lifelong struggle up until that point was, 'Where can I be gay, and actually in a marriage, and a Christian at the same time?' It has put the stamp of approval on my life.

Ben Bell, 50, is the Rector of St George the Martyr, Southwark, London, where he recently ran a Being With course.
None of us were sure what to expect before we began the Being With course. The participants were people who had just started attending or were on the fringes of church life. But from week one, we developed a culture of trust. What stood out most for people was having a safe space that doesn't exist anywhere else in their lives, where they could tell their story and be listened to.

Pretty much all the people who participated have massively increased how much they attend on Sundays. Many of them are now on rotas – they're on the welcome team, doing readings, leading intercessions. As a tool for drawing people into the church community, it's amazing. It brought people from the fringes to the centre of church life – some because they were on a theological journey, others because they were searching for belonging.

In one of our sessions, as we discussed the heart of our week, a participant told us about an amazing work trip to Tokyo. Alongside that, a woman who had had her arms and legs amputated was talking about getting a new front door in her flat that she was able to open herself, and how it had given her back freedoms that she previously had. It gave a number of us a new perspective, and a sense of gratitude for our own situation. But it also felt like a really sacred space where both of those stories were equally valid and were held alongside each other, not in tension necessarily, just held together. Where else would these stories be held together in that way? It's very rare.

Being With is a tool that strongly aligns with my own theology. The course is not old-school catechesis – it doesn't break everything down and explain it systematically. The way it helps nurture faith is subtle and mysterious. I think people's faith has grown more in their hearts than in their heads, and I'm not sure they'd be able to explain it. But it's brilliant, and we'll definitely run it again.

Anna Olson is a priest in the US Episcopal Church in the Diocese of Washington. She has run two Being With courses.
Having been ordained for 24 years and served a variety of congregations, one of the challenges has been finding a pre-packaged course that can work when people bring a lot of different life experiences.

It was a beautiful experience running a Being With Course. I was impressed with the way the course allowed a diverse group of participants to talk to each other in a meaningful way and share things about their lives. At the end of the course, if any of those people ended up in a room together, they would immediately feel they had someone who understood them as a person. That's a lot to ask of a ten-week course.

People quickly started sharing significant experiences in their lives but the container that the course created to hold those things meant that it didn't just feel like people spilling their pain all over the place. We were able to be there with each other as people shared important things and then let everybody go home in one piece.

I do a fair amount of thinking about the gospel message and how it connects to life, but it drew things out of me that I would not have thought of on my own. It works on two levels: there are things that people say out loud, and it also helps us to make sense of things in our lives that we may not necessarily want to talk to the group about.

It's difficult to get people to commit to ten weeks. That's both a challenge and a reason that the course is helpful; congregations need ways to remember why it's worth being connected to each other.

In our diocese, we recently had a complicated conversation about reparations relating to slavery and segregation. It can be a hard thing to talk about and we used the Being With format. We came up with two really simple wonderings: 'I wonder what it's like when something has been broken and can't be fixed', and, 'Tell me about a time when you have either made or received amends.' Then we did a talk about the spiritual and Christian foundations for the approach that we're taking around reparations in our diocese before opening it up for conversation. It has been a really powerful way of having the conversation and has enabled us to think differently about how we talk and behave towards each other in the context of the work that we're doing and as we try to grow together in faith.

Rob Glenny is vicar of three parish churches in Oxfordshire. He has led four Being With courses.
Being With offers participants an insight into a way of being and living that's seldom articulated and very captivating.

If you can experience being with God on a zoom call by hearing your wondering reflected through a talk and bringing the wisdom of the Bible all into one place, that's the whole of the Christian life right there. We want participants to feel it's such a true experience of them and of God that they want to find other places where they can experience that.

Being With doesn't give people all the answers. It leaves them wanting more and, hopefully, we're able to meet that need. Some people have been baptized or confirmed at the end of the course, so it's left them with a desire to make a formal commitment to engaging with church, and an understanding of who God is and how that makes an impact on their lives.

I've been waiting for Being With my whole ministry. I love it because it's the theology I live my life by and that I've committed to living out in public ministry. To have a course that puts that into words better than I can is incredibly helpful.

We try to narrate the ways in which the Holy Spirit has been present in participants' lives until that point and help them see how they have been gently nudged towards worship and a relationship with God. So each course is an opportunity to encounter how God has been at work in the world. As a leader, that is unbelievably precious; it's very affirming for one's own faith and journey, and it never gets boring. I could do a Being With course every week throughout the year and I wouldn't lose interest in it.

Andy Salmon has been Vicar of Sacred Trinity Church, Salford, Manchester, for 20 years. He has run two Being With courses and led training for churches looking to run their own courses.
We're quite a small church, a bit off the beaten track. We average between 30 and 40 people on a Sunday morning and 10 to 20 on Sunday evening. Our congregation is predominantly young adults.

The first time we ran a Being With course, one of our congregation hated it and thought it was a waste of time. He offered to ask everyone who'd done it what they thought, and they all loved it. He'd wanted much more of a sense of 'Here are the answers'. But Being With doesn't offer that. It offers a chance to explore together where God is at work in our lives.

I love it, and my sense is other people love it because it values them and their stories. By the second week, people are talking about the toxic relationship they'd had to get out of, or their mental health struggles. This is a group of strangers – yet there is enough trust that people are willing to share quite deep and important parts of their lives that would normally be hidden. People value being in a safe community.

It gives me a way into people's lives that I wouldn't otherwise have, in that people in my congregation are sharing things that help me better understand them.

It has definitely had an impact on the congregation. Three people recently got confirmed here after doing Being With. Two of them wanted to try and reconnect with church, having grown up Roman Catholic. They liked us and got more involved through Being With. Another had turned up one week and said, 'I've never gone to church, but I feel like there's something missing in my life and I want to find out what it is.'

I'm quite evangelical about Being With. It's a really useful tool and will definitely appeal to people who would not want the more traditional enquirers' groups.

Mark Adams is Vicar of St Margaret's Church, Barking in East London, a historic parish church on the site of an ancient abbey. He has run two Being With courses.
Our congregation is pretty diverse, both ethnically and in that there is a wide range of ages. Our numbers fluctuate between about 80 and 110 on a Sunday. Theologically, it's central Church of England, and that's pretty much where I sit. I come from an evangelical background but, like many people, I've got a few questions about all that now, which is partly why I started doing Being With.

Those who have been in the church for years and have done the course said, 'Well, we've never been asked to think about this before or think about it like this.' It stretches people and challenges them to go deeper in their faith.

It's a good course; it has been positive for people in my congregation, and we will definitely run it again. It offers people a different sort of theology, and they appreciate being given the opportunity to think about things in a fresh way.

It also gives us a common language for, or a common understanding of, the importance of relationships and being with other people for our faith. It has helped some members of my church to see the role that plays in the outworking of our collective faith as a church.

You've definitely got to be comfortable with silence to do Being With. It gives people a lot more time than other courses I've run. It continues the conversation a lot longer and makes it ongoing.

What it also does well is to build trust within the group, which makes it possible to have conversations that would not happen otherwise. On both courses, the groups bonded well, and that meant people really opened up on things that they were dealing with in their own lives; it got them talking about things that they didn't think they were going to talk about.

We got very positive feedback at the end of the course. People were really keen to carry it on.

BEING WITH

Being With has had an impact on my own spiritual outlook and it's affected my preaching as well. It's part of an ongoing journey for me.

I feel it fits with the journey of faith that I've been on and sits much more comfortably with where I am now. I like the relational emphasis, the theology that sits behind it and the primacy of the idea that God in Jesus has come to be with us. That has informed a lot of my thinking.

Andrea Farley is canon for discipleship in the Episcopal Diocese of Spokane in Washington State. She has run two Being With courses for Christians who are themselves interested in running courses, and plans to run one for people who are 'Christian-curious' in the future.

I feel I can really trust the theological framework of Being With. I just love that it revolves around the premise that God's ultimate purpose is to be with us in the most present, tactile, involved way imaginable, and that we are called to join in, both in terms of being with God and being with ourselves and others. It's good theology and non-theological language, so it's something that people can understand.

Allison Moore is an Episcopal priest in the rural community of New Paltz, New York State. Her parish church is adjacent to a university campus. She ran her first Being With course in 2024.

My congregation includes a lot of retired academics and academic librarians; they like worship and outreach but I think they feel they've studied enough and are somewhat resistant to adult education. But a friend of mine was participating in a Being With course and said, 'This is different. This is having people talk to each other.' So, we decided to do a course in person.

For a good three weeks, the talkative people talked a lot, some other folks were pretty quiet, and two people were silent. But, as the time went on, the pace of the exchanges slowed and, by the end, everyone was participating fully.

One of the quieter people on our Being With course said after a few weeks that she'd never talked as much in any group as she did in that class.

Every week people showed up and were excited. These are theologically educated people, and they were really playing with this new take on Jesus' suffering and on the Trinity, and connecting it to their own lives in a way that is authentic.

I also liked the idea that building community is, in itself, a theological practice. I knew that in theory but the way the class helps you structure it means that over time there is an intentional practice about building community that takes on an energy of its own.

Being With is a tool I'm excited about.

Anne Curtis is a physicist and former teacher. She has been a curate with the United Benefice of Radley, Sunningwell and Kennington in Oxfordshire since 2020.

I was ordained in 2020 but my journey to ordination started well before that. After university, I lived and worked in the north of Kenya for a year in an environment where we didn't have a common language or background, or anything. That's where I first learnt that you just deal with the person in front of you as best you can and be attentive to them. But I didn't have a language to put round that before Being With.

Being With offers freedom to explore faith in the context of your own life experiences; there are no right or wrong answers and there's a total acceptance of anything you might want to bring. That can be profoundly healing.

Being With has enabled me, as the leader, to be with people as they open up and explore deep topics safely. I've taken it into my wider ministry, and I use those skills in my entire life now.

References and Further Reading

Richard Adams, *Watership Down* (London: Rex Collings, 1972; Puffin, 2018).
Jerome Berryman, *Godly Play: An Imaginative Approach to Religious Education* (Minneapolis, MN: Augsburg Fortress, 1995).
Sofia Cavalletti, *The Religious Potential of the Child: Experiencing Scripture and Liturgy with Young Children* (Chicago, IL: Liturgy Training Publications, 1992).
Keith Johnstone, *Impro: Improvisation in the Theatre* (London: Methuen, 1981).
Ched Myers, *Binding the Strong Man: A Political Reading of Mark's Story of Jesus*, Twentieth Anniversary Edition (Maryknoll, NY: Orbis Books, 2008).
Samuel Wells, *A Cross in the Heart of God: Reflections on the Death of Jesus* (Norwich: Canterbury Press, 2020).
—— *A Future Bigger than the Past: Catalysing Kingdom Communities* (Norwich: Canterbury Press, 2019).
—— *God's Companions: Reimagining Christian Ethics* (Oxford: Blackwell, 2006).
—— *Hanging by a Thread: The Questions of the Cross* (Norwich: Canterbury Press, 2016 and New York: Church Publishing, 2017).
—— *The Heart of it All: The Bible's Big Picture* (Norwich: Canterbury Press, 2019).
—— *Improvisation: The Drama of Christian Ethics* (London: SPCK and Grand Rapids, MI: Brazos, 2004; 2nd edn, Grand Rapids, MI: Baker, 2018).
—— *Incarnational Ministry: Being with the Church* (Norwich: Canterbury Press and Grand Rapids, MI: Eerdmans, 2017).
—— *Incarnational Mission: Being with the World* (Norwich: Canterbury Press and Grand Rapids, MI: Eerdmans, 2018).
—— *A Nazareth Manifesto: Being with God* (Oxford: Wiley-Blackwell, 2015).

REFERENCES AND FURTHER READING

—— *Speaking the Truth: Preaching in a Pluralistic Culture* (Nashville, TN: Abingdon Press, 2008); rev. edn, *Speaking the Truth: Preaching in a Diverse Culture* (Norwich: Canterbury Press, 2018).

—— *Walk Humbly: Encouragements for Living, Working, and Being* (Norwich: Canterbury Press and Grand Rapids, MI: Eerdmans, 2019).

www.ingramcontent.com/pod-product-compliance
Lightning Source LLC
Chambersburg PA
CBHW060607080526
44585CB00013B/716